IS MY HUSBAND BISEXUAL?

PICTURE

Is He Having an Affair?

By
KAREN WINTERLE

ISBN: 1482565544

ISBN 13: 9781482565546

Library of Congress Control Number: 2014906439

LCCN Imprint Name: **City and State (If applicable)**

DEDICATION

To women suffering the trauma of finding out their partner is bisexual. You are not alone. This book is also for those who suspect their partner might be having an affair or in a ménage a trois. Gaslighting is also a theme in this book. This term comes from the movie "Gaslight" where a husband systematically manipulates his wife to make her feel crazy.

To Mary, my client, who encouraged me to write her story.

DISCLAIMER

This book is not intended to harm anyone. No incidents in this book are presented to inflict damage on any one person or persons. The author cannot be held responsible for any errors. No liability is assumed for damages resulting from the use of the information contained in this book. This book is written solely as a self-help book. The intent is to inform and educate and to help the reader assess a relationship.

Contents

1
Journal Entry of Pain

Mary, my client, brought with her the following journal entry written during the night to her first counseling session.

October 15

You cannot even begin to imagine the pain of finding out your partner is bisexual unless you are in the same situation. How do you describe how you feel? You feel as though the largest crane you can imagine has just ripped your heart from your chest.

You feel numb, as though you are dead and just going through the motions of living. You wonder why you are still alive. Your brain is in fast-forward as you try to make sense of the abomination that has just occurred. Your head aches; inside it feels as if a horrific train collision has occurred. Since you no longer have a heart, you certainly have no soul. Life has ceased to exist. Dreams are no longer a part of life.

Your voice is gone because you cannot put words together to form a sentence. Even if you could, no one wants to hear what you have to say. No one wants to believe this is your reality. No one really understands. The more you try to express yourself in a cry for help, the more your friends and family distance themselves, for you have rocked their perfect world. They do not want to believe that this can happen in their world.

Your eyes want to close, to shut out everything that was associated with your life together as a couple. However, your eyes cannot close, not even long enough to sleep. When you do manage to fall asleep, you jolt awake with flashbacks.

Your legs are barely stable enough to walk through your house that was once a home. Some days you eat; some days you don't. Your friends tell you this will pass. Nevertheless, days go by, months go by, and then a year goes by—or more. You feel as if you are stuck in quicksand, except you do not sink because you do not have the strength to struggle.

You stop listening to music because it reminds you of what you thought had been a good marriage. Memories—both good and bad—engulf you like a tsunami. Sitting and staring are a big part of life now, and emptiness and disbelief consume you. The phone rings, but it requires too much effort to answer it. No one knows that you live in a tomb now. You have died inside, but not quite enough to be laid to rest.

You have ceased to exist.

2
MARY'S STORY

Mary, a client, contacted me for help in coping with a traumatic experience. She had discovered her husband; Jake was in a ménage a trois and a bisexual that was not coming out of the closet. As well, she was a victim of gaslighting. Gaslighting is a term that means manipulating someone by psychological means into questioning themselves by attempting to drive them crazy. Mary was worth over a million dollars dead.

She had just been released from the psychiatric ward at a hospital up north after attempting suicide by putting a rope around her neck, following months of Jake's lies, finding him in bed with another man and gaslighting. She needed a therapist to follow through with the treatment plan.

Mary's brother had given her a ride to her home from the hospital. On Jake's desk was a magazine clipping picturing eight nooses. Obviously, so she would be more successful the next time and to further erode her self esteem. As well as, a bank statement of the joint account they had opened eighteen months prior that she never had access too. Hundreds of thousands of dollars from the insurance claim paid after their business had burned down were supposed to have been deposited. Jake had closed the account the day before Mary attempted suicide. As part of the treatment plan, Mary was leaving Jake and moving to the Florida home. Mary was told to never look back, and have no contact with Jake. Mary packed her belongings into the car. She checked the console for her gun. It was missing. As well, Jake had taken both sets of car keys. Jake was clearly on a mission to destroy Mary for discovering a long time secret of bisexuality and his involvement in a ménage a trois. She remained calm and got a ride to the car dealer, bought a new car, and went to the state police to report her gun missing. She was told it was community property and Jake probably had it. She was scared, Jake now had two guns and a shotgun. She then drove to Florida to start a new life. Jake was continuing to gaslight, erode Mary's self-esteem with the hope she would take her life.

Mary asked me what knowledge I had about affairs, and bisexuals who have not come out of the closet, narcissism, gaslighting and a ménage à trois. I shared with her that I had experience with clients in that situation as well as the skills to help her move through this time in her life. She related that after twelve years of marriage, her world fell apart in a five-month period between April and September. During counseling sessions, Mary shared her story about her discovery of bisexuality. Her partner, Jake, had not—and, she suspects, will never—come out of the closet. Worse, Jake alienated her from her children, family, and her friends accusing her of being a liar.

I told Mary the more Jake assassinated her character, the greater his attempt to hide his bisexuality behind the mask that she never knew existed. Any decent man would never have placed his partner in a shroud of desolation unless he was hiding something. Jake used alienation which is a sign of gaslighting and abuse. As well, he was harboring a lifetime secret lifestyle.

Mary arrived early at my office for her first session. She was conservatively dressed. She had short brown hair and was well groomed, representative of the professional she had been. She was reserved and timid, reminding me of a little girl living inside a fifty-seven-year-old woman's body. The dark shadows under her eyes and her puffy eyelids revealed a woman who was very sad. She carried her own box of tissues for the tears cascading over her cheeks.

Background Information

Mary married Jake twelve years ago—a second marriage for both of them. She was well educated, at the top of the pay scale in her professional career, and loved by everyone. She was attractive, confident, and competent. However, although she was intelligent, she was also quite trusting and naïve with men. Their relationship had seemed perfect; they adored, supported, and respected one another. The world was envious of the love they shared. Every night, they snuggled on the couch, and they were always touching and kissing in private and public. They were best friends, lovers, and confidants and had wonderful, frequent sex. Mary worked Monday through Friday and had flexibility with her hours to accommodate Jake and her children. Mary found Jake to be funny, charismatic, and attractive—a real ladies' man—great partner, stepdad, and friend, he was perfect. Too perfect. Jake was the partner every woman wanted in her life; he was the stepdad who never raised his voice or reprimanded her children. In fact, when they met, Mary's daughters loved him immediately, as did she. Jake was awesome in every way. He was overly generous in giving them money, and he treated her children as if they were gold. Jake quickly became enmeshed with the family and friends. He would later use that enmeshment in alienating Mary.

The family vacationed on the best cruise ships and skied in Vermont every year. They visited Europe and went to the Caribbean. In between vacations, they lived in a country-club setting. Their lovely home up north was on a large lake, and they had a home in Florida. They had the toys: a golf cart, a wave runner, a boat, and much more. She was the breadwinner and made a great deal of money. She worked hard to provide them with a good life.

Jake was a knight in shining armor, and she was his lady. He put Mary on a pedestal, and she reciprocated by providing a life Jake could never have imagined. They frequently danced, fitting into one another's arms as though they were one. Mary was happy to have found someone as adventuresome and romantic as she was. They laughed and talked all the time. Their disagreements were few. They had a good marriage with money, homes, a tight-knit family, and friends. They socialized frequently. She trusted him implicitly. Jake and Mary had just retired, and the golden years were going to be everything they ever dreamed. He waited on her hand and foot and frequently surprised her with flowers and candy.

However, Mary would come to realize at this time that her entire marriage had been a sham.

During Mary's sessions, she told me about the following events that had occurred over a five month period. In April, while in Florida, Jake asked her if she ever thought about participating in a ménage à trois. Mary said no and asked if he had. Jake said he had secrets, didn't she? Mary said no and let the topic drop. A red flag. A week later Jake asked if he could go on a motorcycle trip without her for four days with a younger married couple. The couple was twenty-five years younger than Jake was—in other words, approximately the same age as her adult children. Jake had become acquainted with them in a motorcycle club. Mary asked if the other members of the club were going and

Jake said they didn't want to. Mary thought this request was strange because they had never vacationed apart from one another, but she agreed. In fact, they had been together every day from their first date. I shared that these were red flags. That same month, Jake asked her if she would mind if a third person came to observe them having sex. Mary wouldn't agree. Three red flags in one month.

Mary was not assertive or confrontative with the men that she was intimate with in her life. Jake would become moody when questioned and she learned early on not to rock the boat. She was very trusting and innocent and a peacemaker, a result from significant child abuse by her father. As well as the secrets of molestation by an uncle during her teenage years and rape at 16. Her past led to a lack of assertiveness skills and questioning.

Mary was severely punished by her father and observed her mother and brothers being severely punished. She was hit with a belt regularly, grounded for months at a time, her head banged against walls, thrown up and down stairs, made to eat off the floor, never told I love you, hugged by her parents, touched or kissed and supported. Mary was unloved and unwanted.

I shared bisexuals who want to marry choose women who have low self-esteem, are naïve and aren't confrontative. Mary was perfect for Jake.

She had no freedom to speak up as a child and grew to be an adult that did not speak up with a lover in her life. Her father was controlling, saying no, defending herself or asking what she did wrong was not allowed. No power as a child led to no power as an adult with a lover. Mary used denial and rationalization as coping mechanisms. The same skills she used while married to Jake. This combination made her a magnet for a bisexual relationship. She was a people-pleaser and sensitive to rejection.

In May, Jake said that the length of the trip had changed to five days. She hesitated but agreed to the trip the last week of June. Mary was clearly naïve to what was happening in front of her eyes. The trip was a major sign of an impending ménage à trois.

During the next two months, Jake's behavior began to change. He became short-tempered and withdrawn. Jake started pointing out gay bars and meet up locations for gays. When she asked him how he knew this, he just said, I know. He had always shopped with her, but now he stayed in the car. She would observe him talking on the phone and he would deny it. One night Mary was putting purchases into the car on Jake's s side. Mary saw something shiny on the ground and thinking it was a quarter went to pick it up and Jake had yelled, "Don't touch that." It was a used wet condom. She thought it was strange that it would be there and Jake would know what it was but said nothing.

He began to watch what he ate, lose weight, and exercise. Jake would receive phone calls from the female of the couple he was going away with and always spoke to her when out of Mary's earshot. Occasionally Mary would see him on the phone on the side of the house but never listened in, she respected his privacy. Other times he would say it was a wrong number. A huge red flag.

I shared in gaslighting something is "off" in your life but you can't pinpoint or explain what.

She and Jake had both been divorced ten years when they met. Mary had dated but Jake said he was initially in one eight month relationship, dated outside her species and lived in the black hole. Mary shared that a month into meeting Jake, she asked him if he was gay because he was so perfect. She wondered why he never had relationships with woman, instead he had been attached at the hip to a man for nine years. A huge red flag. Jake had responded, "No, why would you think that?" But something was different about him. He liked to do things woman typically did. Jake told her that he had been into "swinging" for decades with his first wife but would never do that again. Mary thought swinging was wife swapping.

I told Mary that wife swapping is couples exchanging wives for a sexual encounter. Swinging tends to be "anything goes" among consenting adults.

Mary would learn that the term "black hole" meant men secretly meeting up with other men for liaisons. Mary was very innocent to clues of bisexuality. Mary never noticed the clue of his not being with women all those years and that dating outside her species meant seeing men. A red flag.

Mary and Jake were retired and living a wonderful life with many friends and family. They spent winters in Florida and summers up north with beautiful homes in both locations paid for. Mary had been a single mom raising children on her own for ten years prior. She had no family in close proximity. She felt she wanted and needed the love and support of a man; she wanted to love and be loved. Jake was a fantasy come true. Everyone loved him.

On the drive up north, in June, Jake began to have conversations with her about bisexuals. He shared knowledge of the Kinsey scales showing large parts of the population attracted to both sexes. He asked what a man should do if he was sixty-five and had never acted on his true tendencies. Mary told him that she would act on true nature. Jake talked about men coming out of the closet. Mary usually drove, but slept and felt sick to her stomach from the confusion about what was happening. Her gut was telling her something was very wrong.

I told Mary that the American Psychological Association states that sexual orientation falls along a continuum. In other words, someone does not have to be exclusively homosexual or heterosexual but can have varying degrees of both.

Mary asked how someone becomes bisexual.

I explained that although studies are not conclusive, evidence states that brain structure, possible hormonal influences in the womb, and genetics play a factor. In addition, some have suggested that environmental factors affect an individual, such as having a cold and indifferent mother or father or undergoing significant abuse as a child.

After they arrived at their home up north, Mary went into Jake's closet to take his tuxedo shoes out of plastic bags, after a friend had told her they disintegrate fast that way. As she pulled the plastic bag off the shoe, she found a strip of condoms. Jake had quietly come up the stairs and grabbed them from her, saying, "I told you never to go into my closet." Then he abruptly walked away. Jake had a vasectomy, and Mary had her tubes tied. This was another clue of an affair.

The following day, Jake went on a trial motorcycle run with the married couple he would be vacationing with the following week. When he arrived home, he was excited about the good time and said they had talked about sex. Mary and Jake had never discussed sex with anyone else. She felt dumbfounded that he had engaged in such a conversation.

Mary and Jake met with the couple to review the itinerary of the motorcycle vacation. As the male of this couple approached them, he rubbed his hands together as he said to Jake, "A ménage à trois for eight days—doesn't it just make your dick hard?" He repeated it again until Jake nodded his head. Mary sat there perplexed, not believing what she was hearing. This man gave his partner a paper bag and whispered to watch these before they went away. Later Mary would discover they were ménage à trois porn movies.

Mary was then told that the trip was now eight days. When Mary gasped, Jake just yelled at her and said from now on he was in charge of his life, and would do whatever he wanted to do. Then she was told it would be great riding experience for him, she was in shock. This was Jake's fourth motorcycle; he had plenty of riding experience. When Mary asked why the other members of the bike club weren't going, she was told they didn't want to. It was a lie, when Mary later asked them, they were never invited.

From that Thursday until Sunday— when he left for the "experience of a lifetime," the "crème de la crème" vacation, as he referred to it—Jake did not make eye contact or speak to Mary. He avoided her. While Mary had always thought of their vacations as the "experience of a lifetime" or the "crème de la crème," Jake had never used those words with her. Mary never recognized the red flags.

Upon his leaving, Mary began to journal and realized she could go along on the trip by following in the car; then it would be two couples vacationing together. Mary called him, and the other couple agreed. They were at the parent's home of the other couple, who was listening to the conversation.

When Mary met them at the hotel, Jake told her to go home where she belonged. Jake stated this was a trip for three, no more, and that she was not welcome. Mary listened in disbelief, confused by his comment.

I told Mary that he was "gaslighting" her, a tactic of emotional abuse. The abuser ignores agreements and discussions as a part of manipulation. She would learn a lot more about gaslighting throughout the sessions.

The next morning Jake got up and went to breakfast without her, something he had never done. When Mary awoke, Jake was on his motorcycle, ready to leave with the other couple. Mary decided to leave him alone to cool down and agreed to take an alternate route to Luray Caverns. Although Mary left the hotel an hour later, they arrived an hour after that. Jake again told her to go home; she wasn't welcome, he would take her on a nice vacation in the future. Jake was aloof at Luray Caverns. He kept Mary separated from the other couple at the end of the tour group and continually told her that she did not fit in with them. He said it was supposed to be just the three of them. "Three, no more" he would say. Throughout each day, Jake told Mary she was destroying his dream come true. Mary felt numb. Her body and brain were telling her there was something wrong.

Mary stayed with them the rest of the week and watched her relationship deteriorate in front of her eyes. Jake's temper became increasingly horrific. He flirted with the woman of the married couple. He complimented the female on her hair and the outfit she was wearing. Then he would say to Mary, "Why don't you wear clothes like this or let your hair grown long." No one talked to

Mary. The male asked Mary if she ever heard of the movie *Brokeback Mountain*, a movie about two men having an affair who at times go away together, leaving their partners at home. Then he said to Mary, "Figure it out."

Jake continued to belittle her by saying she was disgusting, stupid, and pitiful. He yelled at Mary, "You must have somewhere else to be." Jake told her she needed new friends. They had always shared the same friends. One time Jake got so angry, he shoved Mary while saying she was pathetic. Another time, Jake spit in her face and said he would have hit her had they been alone. Jake would leave for dinner without telling Mary. He called her a liar for saying he could go away on a weeklong vacation and then come along. The degradation and abuse continued all week. Jake had never spoken or acted this way.

The threesome were very angry that Mary stayed and was ruining their vacation. The other couple ignored her.

I shared that the cycle of abuse had begun. Mary was not aware that Jake was abusing her.

She was falling apart emotionally and could not grasp what was happening in front of her eyes. Sometimes the threesome would send Mary ahead of them and go on separate motorcycle runs. She would pull over to the side of the road, hysterical. Once she waited with fear and panic three hours for their arrival, fearing something had happened to them. He didn't answer his phone. When they arrived, Jake said they went on an awesome picnic at a secluded lake. He said he took a lot of pictures. When Mary asked to see them, he said, "No, they're mine."

One evening, Mary noticed Jake's toiletry bag was open. Inside was the strip of condoms. She disregarded this in disbelief.

Mary was using denial, the action of declaring something is not true, refusing to admit the truth or reality of something unpleasant. In psychology, denial is a defense mechanism in which confrontation with a personal problem or with reality is avoided by denying the existence of a problem or reality.

Mary thought Jake was having a nervous breakdown and would not abandon him in this time of need. Her marriage was the most important thing in the world to her.

Jake stopped showing any compassion or empathy for her. A week earlier, Jake had stated that he was now in "control" of his own life. Not that Mary was controlling. However, during this trip, the female of the couple was in complete charge. The female had booked all adjoining rooms for the trip which Mary thought was strange. Jake gruffly told Mary to keep her mouth shut because the other woman was the one in control. Jake had never before told her to shut up.

In a ménage à trois with one woman and two men, the woman is usually in control.

He was using power and control to abuse her. He was alienating Mary to get her out of the picture.

Another time the male of the married couple said he was hungry for a "*sandwich and a happy ending*." Mary thought this was a meal.

I shared it was a term for a ménage à trois.

When they arrived home, Mary confronted Jake. Jake said she had ruined the dream of a lifetime, the crème de la crème by coming along, and he never wanted to talk about it again. He did say he would have nothing to do with this couple again. Then Jake walked out the door. Mary was confused. They never walked out on one another.

He was employing "isolation", a symptom of abuse which lowers self-esteem.

Mary began to share some of the incidents of the trip with long time friends. Considering his changed behavior and aloofness, her friends figured Jake was going through a late midlife crisis. Her friends had suggested Mary encourage him to go for a complete physical and neurological exam. They thought Jake might be a diabetic and that this was causing his edginess and mood swings.

It is now July and Mary is hoping life will return to normal. This couldn't be farther from the truth. Jake's personality had definitely changed. Life would be wonderful for a few days, and then he would have a mood change and the belittling would begin. He would be cold, and yell get out of here, I can't stand you, you make me sick. He would become caustic, erratic and unpredictable. He would say he never loved Mary, he married her as a convenience, and he always loved his first wife and thought they would get back together. Hearing this was like a knife piercing her heart. Mary was riding a merry go round, spinning, trying to make sense of what was happening. As well as, a roller coaster of his highs and lows.

I shared this is part of the cycle of abuse. It can also be characteristics of bipolar. Mostly it was an opportunity for Jake to participate in his ménage a trois.

She kept her belongings in plastic containers and suitcases because she never knew when Jake would go into a rage and force her to leave home. Every other week during that summer, Mary spent two to three nights away in motels sobbing and distraught. She was scared of him. Jake was abusing Mary verbally and occasionally physically until she left the home.

He would welcome Mary back home each week with open arms saying we'll get through this. Life would return to normal with trips to bed and breakfasts, New York City, and socializing with friends. Mary was falling apart bewildered and apprehensive.

That summer Jake would not address her suspicions. He was adamant that he had nothing to do with this couple. However, throughout the day, Jake would walk out the door without saying where he was going. Something he had never done. He had always referred to his first wife as a pathological liar. Mary would learn that Jake was a pathological liar. Other times Jake told Mary she was the most important thing in his life and he could not live without her. Jake would say in September when they are back in Florida, things will be normal again. Mary begged him to go to Florida now but he told her to go alone. She wondered why they had to wait until September.

Mary told me Jake had proposed marriage in four months. A year later they had a fairy tale wedding. Jake felt they should maintain separate checking accounts and continue to file separate income tax returns because his were complicated. Everyone thought Jake owned the business he worked at. Mary never asked him how much he made because she earned a lot of money and she loved him. Huge red flags!

Bisexuals are quick to get engaged and married when they find an innocent, non-confrontative woman. They also look for a woman of means.

Frequently Jake would ask for his name to be added to the deed of Mary's house and she would say sure. You add me to your business. Then he would drop the subject. Well four years after being married Mary was waiting for Jake to close out the register at the business and Jake's mom came up and handed him $400.00. Mary teased her and said how very generous of you. What is the occasion?

She said Jake was the best employee. Jake had lied about owning the business. She used her house for collateral and they bought the business. At that time she saw how little Jake earned. He had lied about his taxes being complicated. Mary never confronted him about any of this.

At this time I shared with Mary that Jake was a narcissist. A narcissist has total disregard for right and wrong. They have a warped sense of superiority, and a lack of empathy. They feel no remorse about hurting others and manipulate for personal gain. Narcissists use lies, deception and charm when attempting to manipulate. When caught in their web of deceit, they become hostile and aggressive. Their lies are calculated. They feel no guilt or shame, they will say or do anything to obtain sympathy or pity, material objects or whatever they want at the moment. They make you feel like you are crazy. Family ties and friendships are severed because of graceful lies by a narcissist. A narcissist moves the relationship quickly in the beginning, making you the center of attention, keeping focus on your wants, needs and desires. All the while feeding you lie after lie. Mary's self esteem, confidence and independence were withering under the flame of gaslighting.

The end of July, while staying in a hotel in Bar Harbor, Maine, after Jake once again forced her out of their home, Jake called Mary at 11:00 P.M.to say her son wanted to know if she was coming home for her grand daughter's birthday. She thought this was strange because her son would have called her for that information and Jake never stayed up past 10:00. Yet he was wide-awake.

I shared Jake wanted her schedule for his liaison.

Mary changed the topic to try to figure out what was going on in their marriage. Jake responded to her pleas in a gruff voice, "You don't know me. You never knew me. You have no idea who I am." Mary was puzzled and cried hysterically as she listened.

Jake then hung up the phone on her, something he had never done. She drifted off to sleep and awoke with a jolt. She thought, "Oh my God, what is he telling me? What don't I know about him?"

Then the floodgates opened. She had filed in her brain all sorts of unusual responses and behaviors since they had met. During those next few hours until daybreak, Mary began journaling in a frenzy of hysterics. It was then that she remembered asking him a month into their relationship if he was "gay'. Jake responding he was into swinging, dated outside her species and was attached at the hip to a man for about 9 years.

Jake always insisted on taking Mondays and Tuesdays off from work. Monday through Friday were the busiest days at his business, yet he took off. She worked Monday and Tuesday. On Monday, he said he went to the movies. On Tuesday, he went to the mall for a coffee and pretzel. What man does this? When Mary asked him what he did during the day, he would excuse himself to the bathroom. Then he would come out with the topic changed. Jake frequently had backside pains, sores in his mouth and sore throats. One time she and Jake met a woman who gave him a big hug and said, "We really miss you, where have you been?" Jake introduced Mary as his wife. However, she and Mary had been neighbors and Mary already knew her. Sharing this with her brother the next day, he said, this isn't good, she's a lesbian and went to the gay bars Jake had pointed out. Another time, a guy came up to Jake, gave him a big hug and also said, "We really miss you. When are you coming down?" Jake said he had no idea what this guy was talking about. He said he didn't know him. Yet this guy called him by his name. In the past month Jake had pointed out numerous gay bars up north.

Sometimes Jake came home with a gleam in his eyes, the gleam he got when they made love. She often wondered about this, but never questioned him. Mary always trusted him. She related that early in their relationship, they had agreed that if either became interested in another person, they would talk about it.

A few times Mary changed her work schedule and stopped by to surprise him at work; his employees would tell her that Jake stepped out or went to town. She thought it was strange that he would leave like that because he was so responsible. Besides, he could send employees on errands. Mary let it go, and that was a big mistake. Her love and trust for Jake kept her from asking Jake what he actually did when he was gone. He was probably using this time for sexual interludes.

Jake suggested Mary wear his bikini underwear to bed. During sex, Jake always needed anal stimulation. Mary said the sex was great from the beginning, but he was controlling, needed the lights out, and preferred rear entry. Jake would ask for anal sex but Mary wasn't into that. Jake's need for anal play was another red flag.

Jake had a flowered swim bag, used women's shaving cream, and had a woman's toiletry bag. Mary always thought this was strange, but Jake's personality pulled this off with his sense of humor and charm. This was another red flag.

She remembered Jake asking her how to delete phone calls and texts on his phone. Then Jake educating her about bisexuals. Finding the strip of condoms, and Jake talking about sex with the couple they barely knew. Jake was walking out of the house daily without saying where he was going.

He had asked her where she kept all of her important papers, who beneficiaries were and what she was worth dead in front of her brothers. She was worth well over a million dollars dead and he was the beneficiary on everything. That month, going through her important papers, she realized they had all been copied and were in disarray. A printout of what happens to an estate if a spouse is admitted to an asylum was there. She froze when she saw this but kept her mouth shut for fear of being thrown out of the house again.

Jake had called the state police one night after Mary touched him. He was told to leave. Mary had found a yellow feather duster in his closet but they didn't dust. And their once active sex life became one time in July. His style of kissing and making love had changed. She recalled asking him why there were tiny hearts all over his butt, the kind you get from whips sold in adult stores. Jake said he didn't know how they got there. He now wore a different style of underwear.

One time she came home after being thrown out and Jake said he stripped the bed and washed the sheets, something he never did, nor would need too. Another time Mary came home unexpected and the grill had been used but Jake hated grilling. Mary asked if he had company, he said no. However, the table next to the grill had only three chairs, instead of the usual four chairs. That night loading the dishwasher she found three plates, three glasses and silverware for three.

Three, no more, from the motorcycle trip echoed in her head. Mary overheard him talking with a man about an alternative lifestyle, and then Jake went away with this person. Stripping the bed one day, something fell under the bed. When Mary looked, there were ménage a trois movies and more in the bedspring. These were major red flags. Yet, Jake denied having contact with the couple.

Then Mary realized the encounters were happening in their home. Mary was out of the picture. Their beautiful, spacious home was available, and the proximity was ideal. This couple lived 6 houses away if you cut through the woods. The couple who participated in the threesome with Jake came in the back door for interludes that took place in every room. Not once did Jake offer to leave the home; he needed their home for his escapades. No one else lived there. Their relationship was no longer his priority. Instead, a young couple had taken her place.

She realized why just three weeks earlier he had gone on a vacation with a couple twenty-five years younger. He had told her it was a trip for just the three of them. The trip wasn't for her. She was not invited. She was not welcome.

"Oh my God," Mary realized, "He is in a ménage à trois! Oh my God, Jake is bisexual!"

Clearly Jake was gaslighting her to get her out of the picture.

Mary called home. When Jake answered, she said, "You're in a ménage à trois. You're bisexual." Jake actually replied, "You are very smart," and then hung up on her again. He did not call back. She had figured it out. However, she didn't want to believe it.

I told Mary "denial" was at work. Denial is a defense mechanism to deny the truth. Jake used a technique known as a "smoke screen", a technique to avoid explanation. Mary made the mistake of rarely asking him to account for his time because she did not want to nag. She was a peacekeeper. Jake hated confrontation, so she avoided it to keep the peace. Women with low self-esteem do not nag or question enough. Accountability is important in an honest relationship. A bisexual partner who does not come out of the closet is usually outgoing and friendly.

Jake liked to wear a bikini bathing suit under a regular bathing suit to the public pool. He would occasionally pull off his suit to reveal his bikini.

I told Mary a sign of "sex addiction" is taking pleasure in exhibiting outrageous behavior. Another sign is multiple sexual partners. Sex addiction is part of the narcissistic personality.

Mary's intuition that something was different about Jake is known as gaydar. This is your gut telling you that he is crossing gender roles. Gaydar is one's intuitive ability to assess others' sexual orientation as gay, bisexual, or heterosexual. Gaydar relies almost exclusively on nonverbal clues, which can include sensitivity to social behaviors and mannerisms. For example, gaydar notices a person's body language or tone of voice when speaking, his or her rejection of gender roles, and his or her occupation and grooming habits. The month Mary met her partner, her gaydar was working. As she shared what was going on with her children, family and friends, no one believed this perfect charming man would do this.

Changing the subject is a tactic used by a gaslighter. This was a big red flag. Malls and movie theaters are popular meet-up places for bisexuals. Jake said he was entitled to these days off. Entitlement is an indicator of "narcissism" (loving oneself above anyone else).

I observed Mary during our sessions. Her breath tightened. She shook. Her teeth clenched. Her body was stiff. Her eyes stared in disbelief. She had difficulty expressing herself and frequently could not retrieve vocabulary to express herself. She was anxious, depressed and having panic attacks. Her psychiatrist gave her prescriptions to cope, but it would be a while before they would be effective.

She threw her clothes into her suitcase and drove home from the hotel to discuss her discovery with him. When confronted, he lied to her, denying her suspicions and refusing to talk about it. Then walked out the door.

Jake was using a tactic known as "minimalizing and denying" another sign of abuse that erodes self-esteem. He was also employing another tactic called "master of the castle".

Then, while he was sleeping, she picked up his cell phone for the first time and checked his phone log. A minute after he had hung up on her, he had called the female of the threesome. There were frequent phone calls and texts between the couple and Jake. Mary was in shock and never addressed this for fear of being thrown out of their home again. Mary felt Jake was supposed to call her back, not one of the threesome. No longer would there be doubt about what he was; she now knew but did not want to believe it.

In August, striping the bed one morning, Mary found three cum stains on his pillow. Upon returning home another time, the comforter in the guestroom was turned sideways, but they had no company. The pillow shams inverted on another bed. Another time she arrived home and found the lawn chairs arranged in three instead of the usual four. He hung a gay pride flag on the back of their boat. One day Mary glanced in his closet and he had placed the females bandanas sticking out from his clothes in plain sight for her to see. These were more clues of him having engaged in a ménage à trois. And major clues of gaslighting. He humiliated Mary at home and in front of others, something he had never done. Red flags poured forth.

I shared Jake wanted her out of the picture. Mary was interfering with his lifestyle and sharing everything that was happening with friends and family to make sense of what was happening. Jake is a narcissist that lies to get what he wants. Her children were confronting him for explanations. He was convincing them that Mary was sick and lying.

I shared Jake had a plan and it didn't include her. Jake was completely enmeshed in a ménage a trois. Gaslighting was taking place by Jake using denial, misdirection, contradiction, and lying. He was attempting to destabilize Mary and delegitimize her beliefs. It is a form of intimidation and psychological abuse. Jake was withholding factual information and providing false information causing a gradual effect of making Mary anxious and confused. She was falling apart.

No matter what she did it was the wrong thing.

When Mary's children confronted Jake, he told them, "Your mother planted the condoms in my shoes." Jake told her children she was not invited on the motorcycle trip because she did not like riding on the back of the bike. (Yet Mary could drive a motorcycle and chose the perfect motorcycle for both of them for excursions.) Another time, they asked him why Mary was not invited on the motorcycle trip; he changed his story and said she did not want to go. Regarding the sheet of nooses, he said that he wanted to learn how to tie knots. He told them that the feminine bandanas sticking out from clothes were rags. Yet they were pink and aqua bandanas. When they asked him if he was having an affair, he said he never made love to another woman.

Sex addicts do not make love to another. They have sex.

He explained the clippings of trips on his desk that he had taken that summer by saying that Mary did not want to go. When they asked why Mary was at hotels each week, he said he did not know. She took off. Yet he had banished her from the home. They questioned his need for copies of deeds, insurance policies, pensions, wills and IRAs; he said he deserved copies in case something happened to Mary. When questioned about all the ménage à trois movies that were in the house, Jake said Mary bought them. He explained going on vacation with a man by saying he wanted to show him around New York and it would just be the two of them. She was not invited. About the guest beds that Mary thought had been slept in, he said she was imagining things. Yet Mary was a perfectionist and everything was always in perfect order. When questioned about outdoor furniture arranged in a setting of three, he said Mary did that and did not remember. When questioned whether he was still involved with the couple from the ménage à trois, he said, no. When questioned about three spots on the pillow from a sexual ejaculation, he said they must have always been there. Jake had a lie for everything.

Meanwhile her friends no longer called her, her children didn't believe her. Jake was discrediting her by making others think she was crazy, irrational and unstable a tactic of gaslighting and a narcissist. Mary continually felt threatened and on edge around Jake. He continually said Mary was to blame for the marriage falling apart. Mary was depressed, isolated, helpless, hopeless and misunderstood. Jake said that Mary was crazy, hallucinating, and psychotic.

The man she had trusted was now a stranger to her. Love was fading to fear. Her mind was spinning with chaos. What had happened? A once loving partner had become cold and indifferent. He had always said, "It's just you and me." Now he was quickly becoming the villain.

Paranoia became the breeding ground in their home. This unfolding drama was very real and destroying what she loved most in the world. Mary was losing Jake to another world about which she knew little. He became vicious; he continually told her how pathetic and disgusting she was. She fell apart daily, sobbing and groveling on the floor for answers that would dispel the reality of her thoughts.

He was using a tactic known as "crazy-making," meaning he was impossible to please, adversarial, nitpicking, and volatile with unreasonable and unpredictable reactionary behavior to get Mary out of the house.

After more than a decade of marriage, Mary discovered Jake was involved in a "*ménage à trois*", where three people sexually interact. There can be one woman and two men, Mary learned, or two women and one man. There can also be three of the same sex.

Mary continued to learn about the dynamics of a ménage à trois (the best of both worlds). The scary part about a ménage à trois is that it can be a secret, deceptive cult when one of the partners is not privy to this. The people who engage in this practice thrive on deception and will do anything to destroy the partner who discovers the affair. They operate like the three musketeers, one for all and all for one. The three begin to speak in terms of us and do not speak to outsiders alone for fear of messing up their story. Hiding such behavior from the partner who does not participate is an adrenaline high for them, further exciting them in their sexual liaisons. Mary had become both the enemy and the victim.

That summer, life continued to be a nightmare. Once Mary said she had a vaginal infection, and Jake immediately went out the door probably to the couple's home instead of sharing concern. Through all of the badgering, Mary persisted in believing the dream that life would return to normal, but to no avail. They made love once in two months. Jake had a high sex drive that was being satisfied elsewhere. These were signs of an affair.

Mary cried as she told me that her life was like a roller coaster. Jake would welcome her home with open arms and the promise that they would get through this. Then the "badgering" would begin again, and Jake would force her out of the home.

This practice is called "distortion", a term that means creating lies and deceptions with a modicum of truth, which makes it difficult to discern what is true and what is not true. Mary was learning about the quiet form of abuse that occurred in her life.

In Mary's absence, Jake told friends, her children, and family that Mary needed psychological help for being so distraught and the severe mood swings. When in fact Jake was the one with severe mood swings. Three years into being with Jake, Mary went into a depression and was diagnosed with bi-polar because her father was. She faithfully took her medication and never had another problem with depression. Jake told friends and family that Mary was overmedicating or not taking her medication and getting drunk abusing alcohol. Jake was using this diagnosis to explain away all the facts that Mary was sharing to his advantage. He shared the bi-polar was out of control. In fact, Mary was out of control but a direct result of gaslighting, narcissism and discovering bisexuality. A year into Mary's treatment plan that included intense therapy, she stopped taking her pill for bi-polar because she was not moving through the stages of grief to anger. She was stuck in shock and depression. She had been misdiagnosed.

Longtime friends and family believed Jake. He would say he didn't know where Mary was, but she called him frequently and shared where she was. He was encouraging friends and family to side with him and succeeding. Jake was loved by everyone with his charming personality.

Closet bisexuals quickly become enmeshed in your family knowing one day their secret may be discovered. They can be the life of the party. This is a tactic closet bisexuals use in case their secret is discovered. No one believed that Jake was having an affair. He blamed Mary and all her friends and family blamed Mary. They were convinced Mary was psychotic, lying and hallucinating.

That summer Mary went to her psychiatrist frequently because her depression and anxiety were out of control. The problem was the new medication couldn't keep up with the discoveries Mary was finding, depression, and anxiety. Mary now had no friends, no family, no support system. When Mary shared what was happening, Jake called her a liar. Who would believe that this was happening to Mary. It was so bizarre.

Jake frequently left the house without any reason. Then he came home later and was congenial. In the "cycle of despair", you work at keeping the peace to rebuild your relationship, and then fear abounds again. Jake did not want to lose the perfect cover. If you are walking on eggshells, emotional abuse is occurring.

Communication was weaker that summer than usual because Mary was afraid of Jake. If she did speak up, she received the silent treatment, evicted, or was locked out of the bedroom. Sometimes he put pillows down the center of the bed so she knew her place. Jake made her feel stupid.

During the summer of her discovery, Jake verbally hurt her relentlessly. Jake found fault with everything Mary did and blamed her for any unhappiness. He used a loud, accusatory voice; intimidation had become a way of life. Jake said that she was the problem. "*Blaming*" and "*intimidation*" are signs of mental abuse. Brochures from trips he took while she was gone appeared on his desk to further erode self-esteem.

They had a grinder pump that grinds all sewage to shoot through a two inch tube. Mary told Jake condoms float. Meanwhile she had taken two of the five screws that held the lid on and left them off. A few days later all five screws were on. She told Jake she had HPV, a lie, and he left the house to share with the couple instead of giving compassion.

Mary shared her trauma with her brothers. They encouraged her to leave, fearing for her life. They knew something was wrong because Jake was always the life of the party. Now he was yelling at her in front of them, irritable, and then walking out the door.

One day Jake took her for a car ride and showed Mary an all-nude resort. Then he asked her if she would like to stay there. Mary found out it was a place were swinging occurred. Later she would realize that is where Jake and his first wife frequented. Jake would point out local gay bars, some in very secluded places, that he was familiar with from the seventies and where to park a car so it would not be noticed. Mary was numb. Who would know this?

Throughout the summer, crying with helplessness, Mary begged for his affection. She begged him to go to couples counseling or go back to Florida. He refused. Jake told her she was crazy and should go live somewhere else. However, Jake never went to live anywhere else. Jake was not going to give up his threesome. He was a sex addict and bisexual who was not coming out of the closet. He was also a narcissist who believed he deserved this pleasure. I heard panic and paranoia in her voice as she told me her story, symptoms of "post-traumatic stress disorder".

Jake told Mary that he had called the state police because she was harassing him and talking about the couple. She said she drove on highways and back roads late at night with no destination, hysterical. Mary was scared the state police would find her. She felt like a felon on the run. She slept in rest areas exhausted from crying and fearful the state police would find her.

Later that August, Jake told Mary to apologize to the couple for all the things she had said about them. In an effort to make peace, Mary went to their house. They told her they would only talk to her if Jake was there. Mary's reality was quickly crumbling.

Later that day, Mary was reading on the back deck. A state trooper arrived and Mary apologized for not turning herself in. He said they had never been called, that Jake had lied. He said he just spoken to the three of them and told me to pack my bags, take the car, go to Florida and never look back. He said he was afraid for my life, and Jake was a very sick man. Mary just sobbed in disbelief.

Physically, Mary was a mess. She was picking at her face, anxiety and depression were out of control. She had gained weight, eating the feelings she was unable to express along the way. Eating filled the void in her now empty marriage. Food offered comfort and an escape. She also started to smoke to numb the pain inside her.

She again confronted Jake about their failing marriage and where he would live. He told her the black hole as he did before he met her. Jake had most likely been having interludes with other men for decades.

For Mary, this situation was incomprehensible, and her realization would haunt her life for many years. During each session, I educated Mary about her bisexual partner who chose to stay in the closet, narcissism, ménage a trois's and gaslighting.

All summer, Mary shared her suspicions regarding her partner with friends and adult children, hoping to get some support. When Mary first began talking about her concerns regarding her partner's behavior, her friends were sympathetic. They soon sided with him, because they did not actually see what was happening behind closed doors. What Mary was sharing seemed so bizarre. She then had to deal with her so-called "insanity" by herself, abandoned by her support system. Her friends from decades before she met Jake abandoned her because his character assassination of lies was so clever. When asked where Mary was, he said, "She took off in the car." He told them he did not know where she was because Mary was crazy. In fact, he brutalized her until she left the house. This was a major symptom of psychological abuse.

That August, as Mary shared with everyone she knew what was happening hoping for support and guidance an acquaintance said, "Didn't you know the female of the couple was a dyke? Look at her. I thought everyone knew." Another warned her to keep Jake away from this couple because they were into some kinky stuff. Another friend that worked with the woman of the couple told her she had to get him away from them. Nevertheless, believing in her partner and committed to marriage, Mary disregarded their comments. She thought they could not live without one another. They were the best thing that ever happened to one another.

After Mary was released from the hospital one acquaintance had said, "Didn't you ever notice how pretty the male of the threesome is?" Another acquaintance said, "They have no friends. There is a reason for that. And the few people they do hang around with are strange." Another friend came forward and said, "I have always known because I met him at a local all-nude resort and was invited to a swinging party. He was a regular." She explained that she never knew how to tell Mary because she knew how much Mary loved him. According to this friend, he answered the door of a house at the all-nude resort—where swingers gathered—in navy silk boxers, drink in hand, and introduced her to his first wife. "Who would know my husband had navy silk boxers?" Mary had asked.

Another friend said she knew he was into threesomes when Mary started dating him, but didn't know how to tell Mary.

Though some friends knew Jake was a closet bisexual, these friends and acquaintances remained silent rather than put a spotlight on their own lives. Another reason was that they become afraid to look at their own families and the possibility of alternative lifestyles. Maybe they did not want to seem nosy or be troublemakers. Some friends may have stayed quiet because they were afraid Mary would not believe them.

When I told Mary that it is estimated that one in ten are lesbian, bisexual, homosexual or transgender, her eyes opened wide as she began to share how that statistic fit into her circle of friends and family. Mary had said, "I never needed the world to know, just me. I would have kept his secret."

Mary's life continued to deteriorate; she was rapidly losing her partner because she had discovered his well-hidden secret life. At the age of sixty-five, Jake's lies were fine-tuned. She would come to realize her partner was a graceful liar, a characteristic of a bisexual who does not come out of the closet and narcissist.

While they were raising the children, Jake was Mr. Nice Guy and she was the bad guy, the one who did all the disciplining. Jake was the silent partner. Mary was the verbal parent. The children ran to him when she grounded them, and Jake listened to them condemn Mary, saying she was crazy. Jake empowered them and formed a solid bond with them, a bond he would use against Mary in alienating her children if she uncovered his hidden life. This bond would make it impossible for her adult children to see her side of what she was revealing to them.

He bought her children's love with generosity. Her children never knew that Jake made much less a year and that she paid for everything they had. Jake and Mary always said, "*We* bought this for you." Mary also introduced Jake to and provided him with a lifestyle he never would have had on his own.

From the beginning Mary never asked Jake how much he made because she was financially secure. When they were buying the business from Jake;s parents, his tax returns were all under $20,000. She was speechless. They took a loan on her house and bought the business together. She added his name to the house. She never saw a tax return again for the store they owned and never signed a tax return. Mary thought this was strange but let it go.

Some bisexuals who do not come out of the closet plan ahead to be taken care of in the event of discovery. They marry a woman of means. Jake felt entitled to these luxuries. He felt special and unique, required excessive admiration and was exploitive, which are signs of narcissism, because he worked so hard at hiding his secret life and so good to Mary and her children.

During sessions, she learned her closet bisexual partner chose well when he picked her. Mary was the perfect cover. She never felt she was good enough with a man; therefore, she was always striving to continue her education to earn more, providing Jake with a lot of free time. He always asked her what her schedule would be so he could plan around it. Mary never asked for accountability. Mary, a real humanitarian, was tolerant and accepting.

Closet bisexuals seek out those who are ignorant of bisexuality. Jake selected Mary because she would be the least likely to ask questions because she was unaware of the lifestyle. Her sympathy, compassion, and understanding were necessary characteristics should circumstances reveal Jake's secret. Following her discovery, his desire was now to turn her world against her, and he succeeded. Besides lies and verbal abuse, he used estrangement of Mary to protect himself.

Closet bisexual partners target women with low self-esteem in relationships, hoping it stays that way. They may choose generous women whose low self-esteem makes it easier for them to maintain their facade and avoid questioning. She was his cover, allowing him to be the perfect heterosexual partner and fit into a heterosexual world so he could fulfill his sex addiction of desiring another.

Mary frequently wrote him letters and left them on the counter, hoping he would see the light and talk to her, begging him, and promising she would be a better wife. She promised him she would lose weight, dress sexy, and always have her hair in place. She would make whatever changes he wanted. He was her soul mate. Now she was realizing he had no soul. She held on to that dream that life would return to normal.

Women with low self-esteem will do anything to make their relationships work. She did not want to be alone, needed love, and would never abandon Jake. After all, he was the most important person in her life. Jake said she was impossible to live with that summer and shared that with her children, family, and friends. This declaration was strange because in the four months prior to the motorcycle trip, they had been on two cruises, hosted a wedding, and continually had overnight guests who stayed for a week at a time. Daily they socialized, hosted dinner parties, and had many friends. Jake had now eroded Mary's self-esteem, self-worth and her world.

Mary told me that Jake never said he was sorry. Instead, she took the blame for everything to keep the peace. His snide looks and contemptuous voice had conditioned her not to question anything. A narcissist sex addict is arrogant and does no wrong. The addict needs excessive admiration and has no conscience.

He had become impossible to live with, demeaning her every moment of the day. Yet Mary held on to the belief that she could make it work, even as their relationship crumbled. Jake had been her best friend, lover, and confidant. Now Jake was stonewalling her—ignoring her, denying events, and barring discussion or acknowledgment.

Prior to her discovery, he made her laugh and was there when she cried. She could tell him anything. Mary had no secrets from him. Jake was a friend with whom she had many adventures. They talked about everything that mattered—or so Mary thought. Mary thought they would be together until "death do us part." She would not learn until much later that Jake was a man in disguise. As her husband verbally and emotionally abused her, Mary wanted to ignore what was right in front of her eyes.

Once Mary began to cease to exist in his life, Jake became a monster—

intimidating, threatening, frightening, and bullying her. Criticizing her eased his guilt. He stopped touching, holding, kissing, and caressing her and became abusive. The pedestal Jake held her on was gone forever. Mary's "happily ever after" was gone.

Confused, one day Mary said to me, "Imagine giving up your relationship so he could enjoy his lifestyle, at my emotional expense, especially when Jake always proclaimed to love me. Who was the man I had married? Where was the man I married?" Jake was a man angered by his lifestyle being uncovered.

Closet bisexual men who marry believe that they can give up desire for men, but it does not happen. Perhaps Jake married her thinking he could change because he loved her so much. He fooled her, friends, and family for all the years of their marriage. Jake wanted to live the American dream, and she gave him that and more. The problem is that bisexual, sex-addicted narcissistic partners who do not come out of the closet are living a lie every day and are forcing themselves to live in a straight world.

Mary needed him to complete her. Mary missed the incredible social life they shared together with friends and a tight-knit family. Mary's need for a man at any expense was codependency. This is putting someone else's needs first.

She was heartbroken because her adult children refused to believe her when she shared her discovery despite all the clues he left behind. They thought he was the good guy.

Clearly, he was gaslighting her with the hope she would take her life, doing a character assassination and abusing Mary psychologically. In domestic violence, the abuser plays mind games. Her children actually believed Jake's lies. He had won the love and respect of her children. The kids now had a birth father and a stepdad, and Mary was an outcast.

Mary lost her mind and support system because of his lies. She rationalized (which was a defense mechanism) that it was down to her to make it work. However, she could not get him to listen to or see her. Yet she could not live without him. Inside her head, she tried to figure out how to compete with men or a couple who were part of his ménage à trois. She thought she could compete if it was just a woman, but how could she be the man he needed in his life? She went to adult stores to buy toys. Then she begged him to help put their relationship back together again. But no one can heal a bisexual.

Mary had read that a ménage à trois could burn out in about six months, which she thought was wonderful because she and Jake could then focus on their relationship. She thought she needed him in her life. How would she survive without him? Desperate to save their relationship, Mary begged to participate in the ménage à trois that summer. Jake said, "You will never be in a ménage à trois. I won't let you." Yet in April, he asked her if she ever thought about it and wanted a third person observe them having sex. Then he stomped out the door with no explanation.

In counseling sessions, Mary came to realize Jake was a compulsive fabricator and was good at it. Narcissist sex-addicted closet bisexual partners have no sense of remorse. A closet bisexual does not change his colors, no matter how much he says he will. Eventually, he goes back to address his needs. He lacks empathy.

Mary shared her suspicions with Jake's brother, who said he had been into swinging in the seventies and eighties but thought he was over that. Jake's brother had been happy when Mary came into his life. His brother said to Jake that Mary "was a keeper and was perfect for him." Perhaps he thought Mary would be the perfect cover for his need for men in his life. Mary hadn't known he was in love with himself in a very selfish way. Jake's brother also referred to him as Dr. Jekyll and Mr. Hyde. Mary always thought that was strange. Now she knew why. She fell right into the trap, hungry for the love of a man who gave her attention.

During the five-month period of this trauma, Mary begged him to come with her to counseling, but he refused to seek outside help. Jake stated Mary's concerns were imaginary and she was to blame for the turmoil. He was scared of exposure. A good therapist would have recognized a narcissistic personality, post-traumatic stress disorder, sex addiction, bi-polar and signs of bisexuality. If Mary had shared her concerns, emotional and psychological abuse would be blatant. Jake stopped comforting her. Others comforted Jake. Mary was interfering with his secret life, and she was a real hindrance to Jake's lifestyle.

One night late in August when she was at a motel after Jake's raging had forced her out; he called her and told her the state police were looking for her and not to come home for at least a week. He would call her and let her know when it was safe to come home. Jake said he hadn't given her phone number or the license plate number, so they wouldn't find her. Mary could hear the other couple in the background chuckling, but she did not want to believe it. Mary sobbed helplessly in disbelief. Scared to death and numb with helplessness and hopelessness.

Once again Jake is up past 10:00 and wide awake. He said the couple he wasn't supposed to be having contact with had brought the state trooper to the house at that hour. He was gaslighting her with all his lies. Mary was on her way to a nervous breakdown.

Instead of staying away Mary decided she needed to catch him in his affair. She went home, parked the car a block away and snuck down to the house to peek in the bedroom window. It took a few nights, then she saw Jake being penetrated by the male of the couple. She heaved and ran, in shock, then went to a hotel for the night. She was numb. Seeing this brought a reality to the nightmare she was living. She never addressed Jake about this. Her coping skills were now non-existent. Denial and rationalization had been replaced by reality and numbness. His gaslighting, driving her to the point of insanity worked. The next day Mary bought a rope to end her life. She called Jake and left a message to tell him she was going to kill herself if he wouldn't talk to her. Jake wasn't home. Mary set the rope up in the garage to jump, state police and an ambulance followed by Jake came down the road. She attempted suicide but was unsuccessful. Mary was admitted to the psych ward.

Mary was still shocked that she stayed, begging and pleading to work through the betrayal that he denied. Mary realized she used denial and rationalization about a lot of what was right in front of her eyes. She learned she had no boundries (a sense of what is right and wrong) as a result of the significant child abuse. She did not know when to walk away.

Mary's children continue to have a very close relationship with Jake. He has convinced them that their mother was the liar about her disclosure of his bisexuality and the ménage a trois, while he was the saint who put up with lies and bizarre behavior in their relationship. He convinced them that she was out of control and abusive. They bought it.

Mary's children, seduced by Jake's suave nature, did not understand that a stepfather removes himself from them when he is separated and gets divorced and spends time with his own children and grandchildren. When he stays actively involved in his former stepchildren's lives, it is because of his gut-wrenching fear of discovery.

Jake still contended that Mary was crazy and made up lies about abuse he endured. What the children did not realize is that the more he is in their lives; the more he is molding them to hate her. Jake needs to do this to keep his secret and the support group he stole from her. They refuse to understand or accept her reality. Jake convinced the children that Mary destroyed a good marriage.

She had a nervous breakdown. Jake never contacted her but did wipe out the checking and savings account. Two of her children visited one night in the psychiatric ward to tell her how much shame she had caused them. She walked away from them. In the psychiatric ward Mary was greeted by her longtime doctor who believed her and said the more Jake belittled her, the more he justified his actions. She began to learn about closet bisexuals, ménage a trois's and gaslighting.

A woman in this situation who feels suicidal should call a friend, family or suicide hotline. She may need to go to a hospital. Most importantly, she needs to seek help!

Jake blaming her and denying an affair, Mary learned, was normal behavior when she discovered his closet bisexuality and a menage a trois. She became his target. Reacting out of fear of discovery, his anger meant to intimidate her. Jake was a master at degradation behind closed doors. Everyone outside closed doors loved him. Mary's children told her that they no longer respected her. They said she was hallucinating and paranoid. They thought she was delusional and psychotic and she needed help for the lies she was telling.

Some bisexual men marry to conform to society. They want long-term relationships and covers. They marry to begin or be in families. These men love their partners. They are great friends and confidants, and they plan to spend the rest of their lives with their partners. Mary's partner was thinking of her when they said their marriage vows; her partner now had the perfect life, but when his secret life was discovered, she became dispensable.

Meanwhile, Jake then went to Florida and turned all of her friends against her saying she was crazy, mentally unstable and a pathological liar. Her daughters stopped talking to her for a few years believing his lies and hating her for making such a character assassination against Jake whom they loved so much. Eight years later and none of her children believe her story. Got to admit, it is outrageous. But years later, the details never deviate. They don't understand closet bisexuality, the strength of a ménage a trois and the insanity of gaslighting or narcisism.

The second week of September, as part of the treatment plan for release, Mary agreed to go to her home in Florida. She had no one talking to her. She got involved in a grief group, anger group, weekly counseling, book clubs and meditation. As well as met me. The anger group didn't work because her medication prevented her from getting angry. This was September of 2011.

Moreover, bisexual partners have double desires and Jake fine-tuned a lifestyle to accommodate the life of a "sex addict" and closet bisexual living in a heterosexual world. Every time Jake forced Mary from their home, he was showing his character and temper, and it gave him the opportunity to commit adultery. He truly was the master of fine-tuned deception.

The rate of attempted suicide among women who find out their partners are bisexual is significant because others are unable to empathize. Straight wives of closet bisexual husbands are walking on foreign land; no one understands this reality.

The first week of October Jake filed a petition for a PFA (protection from abuse order) in Pennsylvania stating Mary was following him in Pennsylvania, New York, Florida and New Jersey. Yet she hadn't been out of the state living in Florida. It was denied. He filed again stating he was fearful for his life because Mary had a gun. Yet Jake had removed her gun when she went into the hospital. Mary had reported it missing to the state police. However Mary had never gotten notification for the hearing and wasn't able to state that. She received notification that she was to stay in Florida 90 days. Jake was free to participate in his ménage a trois without Mary showing up at the house. At the same time Jake filed for spousal support. Jake filed for divorce stating cruel and barbarous treatment and indignities. Mind boggling. Interesting, he wanted spousal support because he said he only had his social security check to live on. Yet he was able to hire the most expensive divorce lawyer.

In November, Jake withdrew his claim for spousal support and went to Brazil with his son for a month. Interesting, he has no money but can afford this.

In December, he filed for spousal support again.

Jake moved to Florida into a house three houses away from Mary. Interesting because the PfA was still in force, yet he had broken it. Her abuser, someone she feared went out of his way to pass her house and speak loudly so she heard his voice. It was a nightmare for her. She suffered from PTSD from all the trauma. He would email, text, send letters and cards to get back together again. He would leave flowers and candy at the front door. Sometimes he would rearrange her outside lawn furniture at her front door to let her know he was thinking of her. And he always drove very slowly past her house. He would come to the main pool or shuffleboard and stare at Mary.

In January, Mary hired a lawyer.

In February, they went to court for spousal support. It was denied because he had cleaned out $100,000.00 from the checking account. Leaving the court house, Jake asked to speak to her and said he had something for her. It was Valentine's Day. Mary's lawyer warned her to stay away from him. A few days later she got a beautiful card in the mail about starting over again and the mistakes made. She did not acknowledge it. In March,

Mary got a long love letter stating if he had it to do all over again, he wouldn't.

Jake once again appealed for spousal support. This time he showed a checking account with $7,000.00 and a social security statement. He was awarded a few thousand a month and arrears.

From the time Mary hired her lawyer, she wanted Jake's phone records. They would show contact with the couple he denied being involved with. Or prove his innocence about Mary's so called character assassination of him. In April, Jake and Mary went to court to subpoena for the sim card and serial number because he refused to turn over the information. Walking into the courtroom Jake handed her another beautiful card about starting all over that she gave to her lawyer. Mary was allowed to give testimony about the trauma she received, When Mary said she wanted the phone, Jake actually stood up and blurted out that Mary had stolen his phone. Which of course was bizarre, since, if Mary had the phone, she would have the phone records. Mary actually thought her children might now side with her, but they didn't. The children actually said the phone records didn't matter. They were so brainwashed.

The following month, in May, Jake was then taking Mary back into court accusing her of slandering him and the couple he was involved with. Jake had Mary's children, Jake's daughter and his brother write character letters against Mary that would be used to tear Mary apart. She was mortified when she read them. They were filled with lies and distortions. They all alluded to Mary being bi-polar and years of paranoia and mood swings that can be a symptom of bi-polar. They all felt Jake should have divorced Mary years ago. The problem with this is that Mary's only symptom was depression and anxiety. They had been convinced by Jake that Mary was off medication and drinking heavily. Jake's brother, who was in their company maybe six times a year, and always briefly, never alone with Mary, stated she had amnesia about conversations, was manipulative, and moody. Jake's daughter stated Mary was unstable and she feared for her father's safety. She stated her brother and she had a stable, loving relationship with their father. Yet her brother had not spoken to Jake from the time Jake filed for divorce. Mary's one daughter stated that Mary had gotten progressively sicker over the past three years. Yet she didn't live at home and stated she had never seen them have an argument. The other daughter stated Mary had always been verbally abusive toward her children. Yet her birth father lived very close and they could have moved in with him at anytime, if this were true. This daughter lived in Florida with her husband. The letters written devastated Mary.

If these letters went to court, Mary's lawyer would have torn them apart. Then showed the cards, letters, as well as texts and emails, not to mention his not obeying the PFA and moving in a house, three houses away would have shown Jake's instability and lies. Mary put together her list of those to testify on her behalf. His parents would testify to his lifestyle of swinging for decades. The lesbian woman they had met that he denied knowing would testify to his swinging at an all-nude resort. The other woman that frequented the all-nude resort would testify to his being into swinging. Members of the motorcycle club that Jake said chose to not come along on the trip the past June would testify that they were never invited. A woman that had shared Jake was into threesomes with a man after the traumatic summer would testify. Jake canceled the new trial.

Along the way, Mary had written numerous property proposals to finalize the divorce. Jake rejected all of them. Clearly, Jake did not want a divorce.

In June, Mary moved back to the Pennsylvania house for the summer. Jake was procrastinating in getting a divorce and Mary thought this would move him along. She lived on the lower level and used the back entrance. Jake frequently washed her clothes and folded them, placing them on her bed. After two years of separation and paying thousands a month in spousal support, Mary's lawyer petitioned the court to force the finality of a divorce. Mary had to pay thousands every month in alimony for three more years, as well as, give Jake a large part of her pension. She took out a mortgage on her house in Florida that she was awarded in the divorce to be able to financially afford to live. Mary lost most of the income she was supposed to have for the rest of her life; Jake robbed her of her dreams and her dignity, family and friends.

At that time, Mary was not moving through the stages of grief to acceptance. The medication for bi-polar was preventing her from moving out of depression into anger. She had been a recluse for two years, with the exception of groups. Mary stopped taking her medication in 2013. She has no symptoms of bi-polar. She had been misdiagnosed. She wonders what Jake, her children and friends would have done if he couldn't use the excuse of bi-polar. Although she reached out to her daughters, they had no contact with her. Jake was still a part of their lives playing poor pitiful Jake.

Three years after the divorce, Jake moved in with a female that lives two blocks away. He still drives slowly past the house.

But his gaslighting, trying to get her to take her life is a trauma she will never forget.

Mary laughs and says do you know my son told me the couple he was involved with got a PFA (protection from abuse) order against Jake for harassment? Then he says why would they do that? I just say you'll never really understand it.

Her daughters came back into her life after two years of abandonment. They never talk about that summer of abuse. It is still a shocking story.

In 2017, the fourth year after her divorce, Mary was making a new will. She was adding her one daughter that is an attorney to her bank accounts. This would open a whole new can of worms. Mary was told she was a member at this new bank since 2010. When she questioned this, the reference was to the joint account she and Jake had opened to deposit all of the money from the fire of their business that Jake ran. Mary's state of mind had returned to the intelligent, vibrant woman she was prior to the 5 months of gaslighting by Jake. Mary requested all bank statements, canceled checks, as well as deposits made by Jake. She would quickly realize that only $300,000.00 had been deposited. Where were the other hundreds of thousands that hadn't been deposited? Of the money deposited, Jake had moved out half of it into other accounts in his own name. She then contacted her divorce lawyer for copies of everything and let her lawyer know that Jake had hidden many assets between 2010 and 2011when they were still together. As a result, she had paid spousal support and alimony for 5 years. Upon receiving the records, she discovered that her lawyer had knowledge of many of these accounts. Yet had not used this information to benefit Mary. Jake had been preparing for a time Mary would discover his secret of bisexuality. Once again, Mary was feeling deceived and betrayal by Jake and now, her lawyer.

She then contacted the insurance company for cancelled checks regarding the claim for the fire that destroyed their business. At this time, she would learn that Jake had never put her name on the policy and couldn't have that information. She often wondered why she never had to sign a tax return for the business but let it go. In case there was doubt as to whether Jake was a narcissist, a liar and cheater, this information was in black and white.

Once again, floodgates opened with epiphanies. Mary would recall how the local fire chief felt the fire started outside the store. Yet Jake and his best friend wanted to meet alone with the insurance adjuster. Mary did meet with them and listened to them express that it was an electrical fire. Mary thought it was strange that his best friend was there but never said anything. She would recall that the business couldn't be sold for retirement because it was losing money every year. Jake felt he would never be able to retire. Then Mary read the newspaper articles about the fire and was blown away that Jake said they planned to retire in April of 2010. Lies. They had a two year plan before retiring. Jake's best friend would say that a fire was the best thing that could happen to the store. Then Jake borrowed $50,000.00 from his father to buy a new car to start retirement off before the checks came in. Mary recalled that they went to his friends house and Jake took the checkbook with him and told Mary to sit in the car. When Jake got back in the car, he threw the checkbook in the glove compartment and said there would never be contact with him again. She thought this was strange but didn't confront him. Another day, one of his employees wanted to collect unemployment and he screamed at her that he has just given her a check for $10,000.00 and never wanted to talk about it again. Mary was perplexed but kept her mouth shut. When they went to buy the new car, Jake told Mary to sit in the car while he took care of the paperwork. Mary would discover that Jake had financed the car when she went through the bank statements, not paid cash, as was the plan. Mary now knew where the $50,000.00 went.

Mary now had to decide if she was going to hire a lawyer and go back into court for the hidden assets. She shared all of this new information with her children. They didn't believe her and another estrangement was pending if she pursued it. So, she dropped it. The relationship with her children and grandchildren was more important to her than the money.

She has not spoken to Jake in years. She journals daily to release feelings from the trauma of being married to a man in disguise and has made a new circle of friends who believe in her. Mary is practicing survival skills and participating in anger, grief, codependency, and self-esteem groups. She has uncovered, discovered and recovered from a marriage that was a sham.

I commend Mary for her resiliency and strength of character to move forward through a horrific trauma that destroyed her sense of self. She works hard to let go of caretaking and instead focuses on loving herself. Mary is learning to put the past behind her. Her children remain connected to Jake because they loved him so much and will probably never see what a graceful liar he is.

Through psychotherapy, Mary became educated about the true motives behind infidelity in her marriage. She has also learned to manage her post-traumatic stress disorder caused by overwhelming betrayal, deception, confusion, and feelings of helplessness. Mary has learned that her low self-esteem with men, codependency, being too trusting, weak assertiveness skills, and naivety caused her to be a magnet for a bisexual partner. In addition, her lack of knowledge about bisexuals, and being too forgiving caused her to be a magnet for a bisexual who wanted to exist in a heterosexual world. Mary also has learned how significant child abuse by her father caused her to become a victim of abuse that continued into her marriage.

The following chapters include summaries of the education, coping skills, and information I presented to Mary. These chapters include helpful hints and information about sex addiction, narcissism, post-traumatic stress disorder, and the grieving process. They also explain survival skills and the cycle of violence, that kept her self-esteem low. I have also included chapters on what she is learning and divorce.

NOTES

PART II

3

CHECKLIST OF AN AFFAIR
(So You Do Not Think You Are Going Crazy)

The following behaviors might indicate your partner is having an affair or in a ménage à trois. It is important to consider the possibility that he may be bisexual.

You will find as you read the following chapter that items are repeated from the previous chapter because I feel they are important in learning about bisexual partners.

____First, and of great importance, is the following statement: If you suspect he is gay, trust your gut.

____Next, when confronting a partner about participating in a ménage à trois or being bisexual, he will tell you he has never "made love" to any woman but you. This is most likely true because bisexuals do not make love. They have sex outside of marriage.

_____He begins to hang out with people who have few heterosexual friends. Be cautious.

_____He begins to point out gay bars. He has knowledge that the typical heterosexual population does not.

_____He suddenly wants to go on vacation with a man, the guys, or a couple without you.

_____He buys new underwear, different from the kind he has always worn.

_____You find condoms hidden in the house even though you as a couple have never used them.

_____His friend tells you your partner once had the largest supply of X-rated movies or magazines in the area.

_____He encourages you to go to adult stores to look at and buy new sex toys, but he never gets around to using them with you.

_____He suddenly suggests separate vacations and encourages you to go away with friends.

_____Your sex life suddenly slows or halts. It may be that is sex desired more often.

_____He is showered and nicely dressed and goes on trips by himself while you have a day planned with other people. He is excited about your day away. When asked what he did all day, he changes the topic or casually walks to another room and says he will be right back. This is a "smoke screen", and partners having affairs are terrific at avoidance. He manages to evade you or becomes angry, refusing to account for his whereabouts. In addition, he always wants to know your schedule and what time you will be home so he can plan his day.

_____He asks you if you ever thought about having a third person watch you have sex.

_____His style of kissing suddenly changes.

_____His style of making love changes, or you feel as if he is just going through the motions.

_____He casually asks if you have ever considered a ménage à trois. He is thinking outside the box of usual behavior!

_____He prefers to have sex with you on your side or from behind, and he prefers sex in the evening with the lights out. Then he needs a finger in his anus to orgasm.

_____He seems to be in a daze while watching TV; his thoughts may be on the men in the show and not on the show itself.

_____His anus is stretched.

_____He gets upset when you initiate sex. He is in control.

_____He tells you that you are not welcome on a trip.

_____He talks to you about men who are coming out and asks, "What do you think a man should do if he is bisexual and hasn't acted on his tendencies?"

_____You find clothing, either for a man or a woman, hidden in his closet that does not belong to either of you.

_____After years of hanging out with the same circle of friends, he says he has outgrown them and becomes friends with people outside your group.

_____You discover bisexual movies or literature hidden. Sex addicts use these to masturbate.

_____He insists he is entitled to days off from work while you work. Entitlement is a strong characteristic of bisexuality, sex addiction, and narcissism. Bisexual partners feel a strong sense of entitlement because they have worked hard at achieving perfect deception.

_____You overhear him talking about an "alternative lifestyle" with another man, and then he changes the topic as you near. He goes on overnight trips with this person.

_____You check his cell phone and notice that many phone calls are from people you do not know. Maybe he starts hiding his cell phone, or he refuses to give you his cell phone records. He may put a lock on his phone so you do not have access.

_____When stripping the bed, you find evidence of sexual activity.

_____He changes bedding in other rooms, even though you have had no overnight guests.

_____He has become caustic, demeaning, and overbearing, forcing you to leave the marital home. This behavior is abuse and a form of violence.

_____You see marks on his body, which might indicate a whip used during his sexual interludes.

_____He is using different aftershave or wearing aftershave.

_____You find a used condom in an unusual place.

_____He hangs a gay pride flag.

_____He starts watching what he eats, exercising, and losing weight to get in shape.

_____He spends time on the phone and only talks when he is out of earshot.

_____He asks you how to delete phone calls from his cell phone. He could be hiding something!

_____He makes your life unbearable with his belittling and hatred.

_____Early into your relationship, friends tell you to stay away from your new partner. Consider their advice!

_____He begins to humiliate you at home and in front of others so much that you sleep in another room. Putting you down gives him an excuse to leave the home.

_____When confronted about having an affair, he tells you that you are crazy, and then he walks away, refusing to talk with you.

_____You tell him that you think he is involved in a ménage à trois, and when giving reasons why you suspect this, he says you are crazy and then walks out the door.

_____He hangs up the phone and says it was a wrong number on a regular basis.

_____He wipes out the checking account. He is leaving. He did not include you in this new plan.

_____He leaves clues and evidence that he is contemplating your demise.

_____You notice a glint in his eyes when he steals a look at the woman or couple with whom you suspect he is involved.

_____After you confront him about working on your relationship, he tells you to go live somewhere else and you are the reason for the problems.

_____In a fury, he admits he never loved you, never wanted to marry you, and only did so because you were a good catch.

_____He takes you for a ride to show you an all-nude resort because "it would be fun" and talks about group sex.

_____After you grovel, cry hysterically, and double over in helplessness, he tells you that you are sick and need psychological help instead of comforting you. Believe him and seek help.

_____He denies having been with the suspected woman, man, or couple and says you are imagining things and are mentally ill.

_____He stops offering compassion or is no longer willing to discuss your concerns.

_____You meet with the person or couple prior to his going away to review the itinerary and are told they have extended the trip and are not welcome. He is making changes to accommodate a new lifestyle.

_____In a call to the state police to report you for making accusations, the officer arrives at your home and tells you that your partner is into some sick stuff. The officer says he is bipolar and that you should pack your bags and get out of his life. Believe him.

_____You confront your partner about your failing marriage and ask him where he will live. He replies, the "black hole." This is living alone to hide secret sexual escapes.

_____Your partner badgers and humiliates you. This is violence to keep your self-esteem low.

_____You overhear him say he is hungry for a "SANDWICH and HAPPY ENDING." This is a term used by participants in a ménage à trois.

_____He loves movies that depict elements of homosexuality, such as *Brokeback Mountain* and *Deliverance*.

_____After you ask him about his having an affair, he says he no longer associates with the person. Then one of the other couple tells you that you were supposed to be gone away; in other words, the other people are privy to information they should not have. He is lying.

_____The couple or person you suspect he is in an affair with knows where you have been and your schedule. They say "we" cannot talk to you unless the third person is present. They are following the sacred rule of the ménage à trois. No one person addresses any concern because the story may become twisted, which can lead to discovery.

_____You attempt to meet with the suspected couple or person, and they call the state police for invading their privacy. Instead of understanding your concern, they are afraid.

_____He tells you he has not been in a relationship for many years prior to meeting you.

_____He suggests you change your hairstyle and grow it long, like the woman with whom you suspect he is having an affair.

_____He suddenly wants you to wear clothing in colors similar to those worn by the other woman you suspect.

_____He asks you if you thought about losing weight. He is belittling you and breaking down your self-esteem.

_____You have suspicions. Check his e-mail messages, telephone, texts, wallet, mileage on his car, and browser history on his computer.

_____He is moody and withdrawn.

_____He treats you like a queen; he may be a queen.

_____He tells you he is going to Fire Island in New York, Montreal, Key West, San Francisco, Cape Cod, Washington, DC, or other cities with significant gay populations.

_____You have been getting vaginal infections since suspicions began.

_____He comes home with sores in his mouth, a sore throat, or backside pains.

_____He carries a plastic clicker in his pocket. It resembles a remote car opener and is used to attract bisexuals.

_____You accidentally find an appointment for a colonoscopy on the desk, and he has not shared concerns with you.

_____He displays clippings of places he would like to visit without you.

_____A friend admits that she first met your partner at a group-sex party. Believe her.

_____You find yourself calling him, begging him, and crying after forced from your home for him to make time for your relationship. He has already decided where the relationship is going.

_____He may have a flowered swim bag or use women's shaving cream. He may use a woman's toiletry bag.

_____His behaviors have become erratic and unpredictable.

_____You feel badgered, shamed, and distraught most of the time.

_____He tells friends and family that you are mentally ill to get them to ally with him and alienate you. He is redirecting the blame to conceal the facts.

_____When he becomes physical, he is totally out of control.

_____If you find yourself dismissing suspicions, be aware of what you are dismissing. This is denial.

_____If he asks how much you are worth dead and where your important papers are in case something happens to you, he may have a plan.

_____He asks you to wear his underwear and may find the idea a turn-on.

_____He actively participates in decorating the house and seems to have better taste than you do.

_____He tells you that you are the only one with the problem.

_____He refuses to accompany you to counseling; he may have a secret and be afraid.

_____Your suspicions make him angry. He may have reacted out of fear of discovery; the anger is meant to intimidate you.

____He refuses to discuss the future of your marriage and says all your concerns are imaginary and your problem. You are in trouble!

____If you feel used and abused, you probably are.

____He finds fault with everything you do. This is his way of further eroding your self-esteem. Keep in mind that he "chose" you because you were perfect for his secret double life. Most likely, you had low self-esteem with men and he came into your life as a knight in shining armor. You are overly understanding, compassionate, and sympathetic. However, you are also very naïve.

____He has begun a character assassination of you. He turns your children, family, and friends against you. He will try to turn your world against you. Alienation is his cover.

____Your life is a roller coaster, and when you are down, it is a merry-go-round.

____During sex, he needs anal stimulation or prefers anal sex. He is not as interested in other typical sexual activities.

_____If your partner insists that you are sick, believe him. You should seek psychological help because he is trying to harm you.

_____He displays extreme homophobic behavior.

_____He reads gay or bisexual literature.

_____If he has a weak sex drive within your relationship, question it.

_____You notice his eyes lingering on other men.

_____You sense he is playing mind games with you.

_____People you have never met approach him, acting as if they have known him a long time, but he does not seem to remember them. They are very surprised he would marry.

_____He describes the Kinsey scale to you, which describes the population of bisexuals, homosexuals, and heterosexuals.

_____At dinner parties, he cleans up and does the dishes, switching gender roles, while you entertain.

_____Men compliment your husband on his clothes or looks.

_____Your husband locks eyes with other men.

_____When your partner shakes hands with other men, he holds their hands a little longer than is expected.

_____He tightly hugs and kisses the men while giving the women only slight pecks on the cheek.

_____Your partner suggests you go to gay clubs because it would be fun and different.

_____Your partner changes his hairstyle.

_____You find a hair in your home that does not belong to you or your partner.

_____He has a passcode on his cell phone or a computer with a pass code and you don't know what it is.

_____He enjoys anal play.

_____He has effeminate mannerisms.

_____He is more sensitive than other men are.

_____He is crossing gender roles.

_____Some bisexual partners cannot handle money and target women with money.

_____Fears dominate your life.

_____You are feeling hopeless and helpless.

_____His personality generates arguments, giving him opportunity to leave the home.

_____He begins to listen to a different kind of music.

_____He wears a bikini bathing suit at inappropriate settings.

_____He is happier than you have seen him in the past. _____His temperament changes.

_____He is working overtime.

_____Your friends, family, or coworkers begin to behave differently around you. It could be that they notice something is amiss.

_____He is on the Internet more than usual.

_____He is slow to become sexually intimate with you.

_____You feel sick to your stomach during a conversation or encounter with him.

_____He begins to wear a different style of clothing.

_____He is suddenly changing bed linen.

_____There are spots of sexual activity where none supposedly took place.

_____His taste in movies changes to include those that depict different types of sexuality.

_____He presents you with unexpected gifts.

_____There is more mileage on the car than has been typical.

_____He is working longer hours than before.

_____He encourages you to go on vacations.

_____He had an affair when he was with his last partner.

There is wonderful user-friendly surveillance equipment on the market, such as remote audio and visual cameras and voice-activated tape recorders. As well, there are GPS apps that can be put on a cell phone to monitor his location. Look online for an array of video surveillance equipment. Car trackers install easily in a magnetic case underneath the car. Buy it now, and use it! Monitor the mileage on his car.

You must go for STD testing if you suspect he is an active bisexual, having an affair or in a ménage a trois.

NOTES

4
LOW SELF-ESTEEM

I have included this chapter because keeping your self-esteem low is necessary for the success of a bisexual living a double life. Your partner most likely does not want to lose you, for you are the one he hides behind to keep his secret. Power and control is his vehicle to keep self-esteem low. His goal is to keep you in your place—passive. The following are tactics and behaviors that abusers use.

Intimidation

If his looks, actions, or gestures frighten you, he is using intimidation, a form of violence. He may intimidate you by doing the following:

- putting you down,
- making you feel bad about yourself,
- making you think you are crazy,
- playing mind games,
- humiliating you, or

- making you feel guilt and shame.

Isolation

This may include him doing the following:

- controlling what you do,
- monitoring who you see and talk to,
- insisting on knowing where you go,
- using jealousy to justify his actions, or
- continually leaving the home.

Minimizing, Denying, and Blaming

If he makes light of the abuse, does not take your concerns seriously, says the abuse did not happen, shifts responsibility for his abusive behavior, and says you caused it, get away from him as soon as possible and seek help.

Using Male Privilege

Ask yourself the following questions:

- Is he defining male and female roles?
- Is he treating you like a servant?
- Is he making all the major decisions?
- Is he acting like a master of the castle?

Economic Abuse

Ask yourself the following questions:

- Does he prevent you from getting or keeping a job?
- Does he make you ask for money?
- Does he give you an allowance?
- Does he take your money?
- Does he limit your access to the family's income?

Using Children

He may be doing the following:

- telling the children you are crazy,

- using the children to relay messages,
- lying to the children,
- making you feel guilty about how they were raised,
- encouraging the children to side with him,
- using visitation to harass,
- threatening to report you to child welfare or the state police, or
- threatening to take the children away.

Coercion and Threats

He makes light of the abuse, does not take your concerns seriously, and says the abuse did not happen, shifts responsibility for his abusive behavior, or says you caused it. Run away as fast as you can.

Cycle of Despair

- You continually work at keeping the peace.

- The relationship then escalates to provocation.
- Violent outbursts shatter your self-esteem.
- You reconcile.
- You rebuild the relationship.
- He minimalizes the issue.
- You gain hope.
- You become protective toward your partner.
- You express needs and demands.
- You have differences of opinion.
- You attempt to humor your partner.
- You are again defensive.
- Fear once again abounds.
- The circle begins again.

Cycle of Violence

- Potential for violence (physical or emotional)
- Trigger(s)
- Violent outbursts
- His regrets
- His becoming "Mr. Nice Guy"

- Reappraisal of your relationship
- Denial and blame when something is wrong again
- Fault-finding
- Tension
- Abuse

Upon your discovery of low self-esteem, it is important not to jump into another relationship because the probability of choosing another bisexual partner is high. Women with low self-esteem are magnets for bisexual men. These women have qualities that make them perfect for the role they will play in their lives. These women put their partners above all else. His happiness is all that matters.

The cycles of despair, violence, power, and control are important to recognize so that you do not become the target of his abuse. His goal is to keep you in your place. He wants to keep you passive.

Seek help to build self-esteem.

NOTES

5
SEX ADDICTION

Throughout psychotherapy, Mary became educated about the world of sex addiction. Bisexual partners can also be sex addicts if acting on their true tendencies. Jake got involved in a ménage à trois, offering the best of both worlds to the bisexual. Bisexuals are attracted to men and women. Bisexual partners are able to compartmentalize, enabling them to live out their secret lives. They box each aspect of their lives, and they open whichever box they need at the time to deal with their internal chaos. Box A, Mary, might represent society, values, and family. In Box A, Jake is the good guy. Box B, on the other hand, includes the other men or women in his life. This box allows him to be his true self or have affairs. In this box, he holds his secret life and addictions.

His rationalizations indicate which box he is in now. For example, if he is criticizing you, making irrational statements to get away or get you away, or if he cannot account for his time away, he is moving toward Box B. Conversely, if he is stating how crazy life would be without you and praising you, then it is Box A. Leading a double life is not too complicated for the bisexual as long as he keeps straight which box he is in at the time. Box B contains his entitlement. Entitlement (narcissism) is a strong characteristic of bisexual partners. He engages regularly in adultery.

He has no moral, spiritual, or emotional maturity. His sexual addiction probably began in his teenage years. The bisexual partner may work hard, be a good neighbor, or see himself through the lens of his goodness. The badness is isolated, contained, and compartmentalized in Box B.

When caught, his bubble is popped. The grandiose (Box B) part of his identity is exposed. The bisexual sex addict then focuses on the partner. To protect himself, he says that she is the one who has issues. This manifests in his anger and rage. He is no longer superior in his partner's eyes. Instead of feeling shame, it is the opposite. He feels infuriated and begins to blame her and accuse her of being crazy.

The sex addict usually has few hobbies and rarely challenges himself. He has no place, where he can take risks. He usually does not participate in or like sports. Sex is his activity; it is his adventure. He gets high on the risk, the unknown, the challenge. He takes pleasure in how to accomplish all of this undetected. When caught, his sense of adventure is lost. He is enraged and directs his fury toward his spouse for that rush of endorphins again.

The sex-addicted partner can also experiment with swinging or a ménage à trois because of his insatiable appetite for sex. He will stray into unfamiliar territory for physical pleasure. Swinging is a non-monogamous activity he treats like any other social activity. It has a recreational perspective. Swinging is like a sport. A sex addict does not make love; he has sex.

Sex addicts, swingers, and participants in a ménage à trois acknowledge sex as a game and participants as teammates.

Exhibitionism and voyeurism are usually part of the game. Exhibitionism, part of the high, is a form of pleasure that involves sex with a partner while being watched by at least one other person. Voyeurism is watching others performing sex. More extreme measures include spanking, bondage, and water sports (that is, urinating on one another).

They love the addiction, the lies, and the excuses. They love sneaking around and being accountable to no one. They are usually unwilling to take a polygraph test and love to masturbate to pornography. They would rather devastate their home lives than give up their sex addictions, which would result in greater pain for them.

They have a sense of arrogance. Mary's partner remained in the closet, which resulted in abusive behavior. Jake was married to his addiction in Box B. Mary became dispensable when she discovered his secret in Box B. She was now outside of his world.

The sex addict negotiates with himself regarding how much addiction he can accommodate while still enjoying the benefits of marriage. His world is one of lies. Mary discovered Jake's indiscretions because he was gluttonous and wanted the ménage à trois, the crème de la crème, and the dream of a lifetime all at once. He also left a trail of clues and got caught. The problem is that the sex addict has a limited ability to love genuinely while fine-tuning his game for a lifestyle of addiction.

When caught, the bisexual sex addict is between two worlds. He attempts to suppress his sexuality to enter the heterosexual world. These ambiguous feelings must surface at some point, so he begins to direct his anger and frustration at his partner behind closed doors. He blames his partner for his confusion and can become mentally or physically abusive. In this way, he keeps his partner's self-esteem low. He forces his partner to be passive. The partner alone cannot satisfy his sexual desires.

The partner is closest to him, and, hence, she is the most secure target, allowing him to lie to her. A partner who discovers the adultery may stay within the idealized society, choosing to look the other way rather than lose her marriage and dream of happily ever after.

The partner of the bisexual addict generally has a personality that fits perfectly into Box A. The partner may be more supportive, understanding, and less demanding than others are, which is what attracts the bisexual man to her. The partner's passive personality may extend to hiding the bisexuality to the outside world when the addiction is revealed.

It took a very long time for Mary to realize and accept that her partner was not truly committed to their relationship. He was committed to the life in a straight world—family, marriage, and the convenience of a partner. At the same time, he was committed to his secret bisexual sex addiction.

Mary's partner had the largest selection of gay magazines in the area as well as the largest supply of gay movies. He used these to satisfy his sex addiction, fantasize, and masturbate.

For the bisexual partner, adultery is not an issue. He sees himself as a good guy. He is a good provider and plays the role of the heterosexual partner perfectly. When the addict is caught, the bad guy hidden in Box B comes out, hitting him hard. When he sees his faithful partner sobbing on the floor, he sees only the bad in her. She has become the ax-murderer of the one person she loved and needed most, and she will do anything to get her "good guy" back again.

Then the real roller coaster begins as the addict begins playing head games. If the partner knows too much of the truth of Box B, the goal is to convince the outside world how very sick she is. The character assassination begins. His way of life becomes engaging the victim, victimizing her, and then exiting. When she discovers the affair, she is the perpetrator of pain. He will impose such indignities as to render her living conditions intolerable. He is guilty of marital misconduct and betrayal. He does not care that he is exposing her to STDs or that she may have a mental breakdown. The sex addict is out to survive at any cost.

The bisexual convinces her and the world that she has been in control in the relationship, and he pretends to lead a life of deprivation, which leads to his sense of entitlement. When he chooses to remain in the closet, he will destroy her for getting in the way of his alternative lifestyle. He will destroy her support system by saying she is mentally ill, hallucinating, and lying. The bisexual addict will humiliate, badger, and degrade her to hide the secret she is trying to expose or for seeking answers for what is happening in her life.

Mary became distraught and lived in a state of unpredictable insanity. She lived in fear when he went into his furies. He could now live peacefully in Box B and save face by destroying Box A (which had held Mary). A sex addict engaging in extramarital affairs is not exactly the paragon of honesty. He will hurt his partner to protect his addiction to other men or women. He is a smooth talker.

NOTES

6
POST-TRAUMATIC STRESS DISORDER

During Mary's discovery, something else was happening inside her body, known as post-traumatic stress disorder (PTSD). This is a condition characterized by nightmares, flashbacks, and feelings of detachment, irritability, trouble concentrating, and sleeplessness. The PTSD sufferer may experience blackouts or have a hard time recalling things. This person may be easily and often startled and be constantly on the lookout for threats. Physical manifestations include constipation, diarrhea, rapid breathing, muscle tension, and rapid heartbeat. For Mary, this trauma was indeed real, and the persistent feelings of shame, guilt, and isolation were real.

The trauma severely compromises the emotional well-being of an individual and causes intense fear. Some may feel the perpetrator of the trauma is all-powerful, that he is preoccupied with revenge. Mary worried constantly feeling loneliness, helplessness, hopelessness, and despair.

Mary had thoughts of suicide. Anyone with such thoughts should seek help immediately.

In addition, those with PTSD should seek help.

A traumatic event is something horrible and scary that you see or that happens to you. During this type of event, you feel afraid and that you have no control over what is happening to you. You may feel scared, confused, and angry. If these feelings do not go away or get worse, you may need medication in addition to therapy.

It is usual to relive the event, which may lead to emotional numbness, hyper-arousal, and avoidance. The emotional numbness may present as a lack of interest in activities that you used to enjoy, distancing yourself from people, or having a sense of a foreshortened future (for example, not being able to think about the future or make future plans or believing you will not live much longer). Depression is also a big part of discovering someone you love is bisexual. Avoidance can occur to the point of having a phobia of places, people, and experiences that remind you of the trauma.

Other symptoms of PTSD include panic attacks, which include feelings of intense fear accompanied by shortness of breath, dizziness, sweating, nausea, and a racing heart.

A therapist will teach you about PTSD. You will need to receive counseling regularly and have the support of a psychiatrist. With new coping skills, you learn to understand the personality of a bisexual partner and work on self-esteem to rebuild life and move beyond the blackness into the light.

NOTES

7
NARCISSISM

Some bisexual men exhibit narcissistic personality traits. The narcissist partner, for example, loves you one moment and belittles you the next. He manipulates you because he really does not want to lose you. The narcissistic bisexual partner may exhibit the following:

- has a strong sense of entitlement;
- has a fear of being inferior;
- has an exaggerated sense of self;
- is self-absorbed;
- wants excessive attention and admiration;
- expects special treatment;
- lacks real empathy;
- brags constantly;
- attacks you if he feels insulted;
- tries to control others to avoid feeling inferior;
- uses seductive charm to get what he wants;

- is unaware of his own risk taking (for example, engaging in sexual liaisons);
- is preoccupied by sexual fantasies;
- targets you;
- repeatedly attacks or blames you, the target, with violence, verbal abuse, and financial and legal abuse;
- sees you as all bad when he is found out;
- has extreme emotional intensity about blaming you;
- launches personal attacks on your intelligence and sanity;
- recruits others to attack you;
- seeks validation for his own thinking and behavior; or
- seeks retaliation;
- lies to get what he wants;
- feels no guilt or shame
- atheist or agnostic, because he is a god;

- doesn't let go of past relationships;

The bisexual narcissist is highly sensitive to criticism and experiences rapid mood swings, sudden anger, impulsive behavior, and potential violence. He has a great fear of abandonment or losing his inflated self-image. At the same time, the narcissistic can be extremely charming, exciting, and persuasive.

Because the bisexual partner is usually, articulate and exudes sexuality, his narcissism gives off energy. It is all about him and his needs. The stench of entitlement is also present in his heart. The bisexual narcissist sex addict is disconnected; he harbors secrets. He lacks true intimacy and has an appetite for fetishes. He will play head games. For example, Mary's partner wrote and put a poem on the coffee table for her to find while denying being in another relationship:

Back on the street again
Back on my feet again

Looking for love
Just two and me
Flying high in the sky.

The narcissist bisexual twists facts to accommodate his needs. If you verbally attack or accuse him, he can become vicious. His goal is then to humiliate you, spread rumors about you, and give himself an excuse to abuse you. Moreover, the narcissist tells you that you are the crazy one and that you are imagining things. He works hard to distort your reality to ensure his safety. He also takes pride in having no flaws and has extreme and illogical sensitivities. He thinks he is perfect and will destroy anyone who threatens his facade. He can become demeaning, demanding, and critical.

He believes he is better than others. He embellishes his achievements, believing he is special. It is all about him. Moreover, he is excessively preoccupied with issues of personal adequacy, power, prestige, and vanity—that is, he is egocentric. He is arrogant and needs attention at all times. Mary learned the narcissistic personality fits into having a sex addiction as well as being a closet Mary lost most of the income she was supposed to have for the rest of her life; Jake robbed her of her dreams and her dignity, family and friends.

A narcissistic individual requires a narcissistic supply from someone. Narcissistic supply is a concept, which describes a type of admiration, interpersonal support or sustenance drawn by an individual from his environment (especially from codependents, love addicts and others). The term does not take into account the feelings, opinions or preferences of other people. If you find yourself feeling drained, tired, depressed, angry or confused you may be in a relationship with a narcissist. Mary was Jake's narcissistic supply. She allowed herself to be controlled by her desperation to be loved. She feared abandonment, needed approval and had a strong desire to please. Mary was constantly surrendering her energy to avoid conflict and further abuse.

Narcissists are talented manipulators, as are sex addicts and closet bisexuals. They will treat you badly because you allow the mistreatment. They look after their own interests first and foremost.

If you realize you are involved with a narcissist, seek professional help.

NOTES

8
SOME POSSIBLE CHARACTERISTICS of BISEXUAL MEN

Disclaimer: Your partner displaying the following characteristics does not necessarily imply he is bisexual.

- Compulsive liar
- Charming
- Masculine-looking
- Egotistical
- Charismatic
- Perfect husband, partner, and father
- Perfect stepfather and friend
- Engaging
- Slow to get involved sexually
- Nurturing, affectionate
- Exuding sexuality and a sense of entitlement
- Having frequent mood swings
- Unable to handle money

- Targeting a woman of means
- Addicted to sex
- Having unaccountable time
- Asking you to account for your time
- Choosing women with low self-esteem (peace-keepers)

NOTES

9
STAGES of GRIEF

The loss has been horrific; you have to do a lot of work to move forward in your life. Your feelings of despair, worthlessness, helplessness, hopelessness, anger, shame, and guilt are overwhelming. When Mary found out she married a bisexual partner, especially one who was a narcissist and sex addict, her life fell apart. Destroyed, she did not want to go on living. She had lost her partner, children, family, and friends within a five-month period.

While grieving, you might sleep all the time or not at all. You may lose your appetite, or it may increase. Nightmares and flashbacks occur frequently. You may feel numb, going through the motions with no emotion. You will mourn, for a death has occurred.

The Kübler-Ross model lists five stages of grief:

- Shock, denial, disbelief, and numbness

- Anger
- Bargaining
- Depression
- Acceptance

Shock/denial: This is a numb place where feelings do not exist. You cannot believe this is happening to you. Your life had been great together. The relationship is over, which is hard for you to grasp.

Anger: You hate your husband; he has destroyed your life. You never want to see him again. Rage and envy invade your life at this stage, but you are moving forward in the process.

Bargaining: You may ask yourself, "Why me?" You tell yourself, "We can make our relationship work." You say, "I will do what is necessary to make this work. We were supposed to be forever. We promised in vows of marriage that through sickness and health, good times and bad times, we would be there for one another until death do us part." You say you will be a better wife. You tell him he won't have to account for his time away. You may want to contact your partner to try to heal the relationship. Do not do it! It will only lead to emotional setbacks.

Depression: You are sad, helpless, and hopeless. You might wish to die or to be at peace. You feel as if you do not have the strength to endure this any longer. You miss your partner and feel you cannot live without him.

Acceptance: You say to yourself, "I am going to survive. I will overcome this nightmare." In this stage, you come to terms with your losses. You laugh now and make plans for your future. The past is over, and a new chapter begins. The bond of betrayal is broken. Life will be better because you have learned lessons along the way from discovery to recovery.

These stages are fluid. The grieving process lasts approximately two years in the loss of a heterosexual relationship. However, finding out you were married to a bisexual, especially one who will never come out of the closet, is monumental. Take your time and realize that eventually you will heal. Feel your feelings. Recognize and honor them so you can move on.

Do not contact him during this process. Your relationship is over. Significant losses have occurred; even worse, these losses may bring to the surface losses you have never dealt with in the past. You have lost the following:

- a marriage
- a soul mate
- financial security
- family
- friends
- the hope of growing old together
- a home
- trust
- honesty in a relationship
- whatever self-esteem you thought you had
- a dream

Luckier is the person whose partner is honest enough to admit his bisexuality. For this person, the process may be shorter. The heart has been shattered into a billion pieces.

The event has been so catastrophic that an individual may never get over the loss.

Letting the process evolve in its own time is important. Wishing it would pass just expends the energy you need to work through the process.

During the grieving process, which may take years, friends and family may tire of hearing you vent the horror. Ignore them. Seek the support of mental health services and support groups. Friends and family might not understand that this breakup is different from the breakup of a heterosexual relationship. Even divorce does not end the pain. The flashbacks may still occur when you least expect it. A song on the radio, for example, may cause you to burst into tears.

During the grieving process, set aside specific hours for grieving during the day and then begin to fill in the spaces with responsibilities and survival skills. Mary grows stronger every day from psychotherapy and through her education. In the years since

Mary's discovery, she has removed herself from toxicity.

NOTES

10
SURVIVAL SKILLS

If you are going to survive this hell, you need a lot of support. Below I have provided a list of ideas:

- Seek counseling.
- Join support groups to address anger, grief, self-esteem, women's issues and codependency (CODA).
- Join a book club for self-growth.
- Ask for support from friends.
- Spend time with family.
- Keep a journal.
- Remember that you are a survivor.
- Allow yourself to discover the new you.
- Turn the page for a new beginning.

- Accept that there will be much darkness before there is light.
- Educate yourself with the latest research.
- Use the library, e-books, and the Internet
- Follow online blogs.
- Meditate and find or renew your faith.
- Take up new hobbies.
- Practice loving yourself by looking in the mirror and saying, "I love you" or "I accept myself just as I am.
- Acknowledge the grieving process.
- Play games.
- Play cards.
- Put puzzles together.
- Draw or paint.
- Get into gardening.
- Exercise, do yoga, or walk.
- Ride a bike.

- Rent comedies.
- Take up scuba diving.
- Learn to golf.
- Do something you have never done.
- List what you are grateful for every day.
- Do affirmations daily.
- Write a list of what you deserve in the future.
- Return to school.
- Make new friends.
- Get a job.
- Take assertiveness training.
- Dig deep into your memory and make a list of positive abilities, hopes, and dreams.
- Remember you are perfect in God's eyes.
- Let go of yesterday, which leads to depression.
- Live only today.

- Do not dwell on tomorrow, which leads to anxiety.

To keep herself from contacting Jake, Mary found it helpful to write a list of her husband's characteristics that she despised. I suggested she picture the word *sick* on his forehead if he contacted her.

NOTES

11
DIVORCE TIPS

Chances are high that when you discover the addict's bisexual secret life, he will file for divorce. Alternatively, you might need to file for divorce because his bisexuality will not go away. He is never going to be heterosexual. Trust and honest communication never occurred in your marriage. Compulsive lying and a lack of conscience are his way of life.

The partner who does not come out of the closet is out to get you. Prepare yourself for the inevitable—war—and take this very seriously. Mary learned the hard way through her naivety. He will come at you with vengeance. He is the hunter out for the kill, and you are the prey. Know the gravity of his wrath. At any time, he could evict you from your home. Jake obtained a protection from abuse (PFA) order from the court for ninety days because Mary was still groveling hysterically in an attempt to work through this horror.

I suggest the following prior to filing for divorce:

____Find a safe place to go.

____Get some ready cash or beat him to the bank to empty the bank accounts. Pay off bills in your name.

____Copy important records and keep them in a safe place. Write down all the details you can recall. Keep a journal of anything pertinent; write down names, dates, and places.

____Check the computer for e-mail messages and copy them. Check the browser history, text messages, and letters. Check the trash folder. You can use this as evidence.

____Take pictures of anything you find suspicious on his computer. If you are unable to find anything incriminating, take the hard drive to a computer expert to look for hidden files or recently deleted folders.

____Keep a notebook in your purse and car to jot down anything you can remember.

____Use financial records. If your partner spent money on an affair, you may be able to use this as evidence. Search the records for vacations, gifts, or other unusual spending. Look for receipts or repeated ATM withdrawals. In the property settlement, you may be entitled to more than half of the assets for a fraudulent marriage.

_____Hire a private investigator. He or she will be able to provide evidence in court.

_____Communicate only through your attorney. If you absolutely must have contact, keep your words minimal. Otherwise, remove yourself. Anything you say may be introduced into evidence. Be very brief in e-mail or texts and copy yourself. Buy an external hard drive or a flash drive and save the copy again.

_____See a counselor, psychiatrist, mental health worker, or social worker to document the pain you are going through. Any of these professionals will then be able to write a report for court.

_____Take out a term life insurance policy on him for as much as you can afford. Term insurance is more affordable. Women usually live longer than men do. Do this especially if you have children. Make sure you are the owner and the beneficiary.

_____Change beneficiaries on life insurance policies to protect any inheritance.

_____If you own property in your name, put it in someone's name that you trust implicitly.

_____Get your own credit cards. Take your name off his credit cards.

_____Open up your own checking account. Then add a joint owner.

_____Invest in spyware for your computers.

_____Buy tape recorders and hide them in his car or in the house to gather as much information as you can against him.

_____Print out phone records to use as proof of marital conduct. If your partner has been chatting with another party, you can use the phone records to help prove your case of adultery.

_____Speak to your divorce attorney about charges of marital misconduct. An attorney will be able to help you with the exact proof required. Many factors are considered when the judge decides on alimony, and marital misconduct is only one of them.

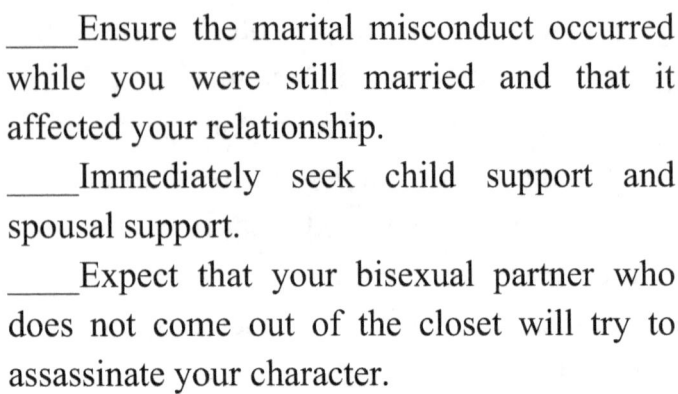

_____Ensure the marital misconduct occurred while you were still married and that it affected your relationship.

_____Immediately seek child support and spousal support.

_____Expect that your bisexual partner who does not come out of the closet will try to assassinate your character.

_____Go through the house with a fine-tooth comb to look for evidence of an affair. Check in box springs and between mattresses and box springs. Take pictures, and have a friend observe any findings.

Make sure your lawyer does a thorough credit check on him that shows all bank accounts and credit cards in his name.

Do not prolong the divorce process. The only people benefiting from prolonging the process are the lawyers. The closet bisexual husband will try to assassinate your character to drag you through the court system to disprove your accusations.

In the end, the divorce is all about the property settlement. Lawyers make it a point of telling you that you will come out with everything without paying him a penny. Do not believe them. After the divorce, spousal support becomes alimony in many states. Usually assets are to be equally distributed. Research equitable distribution, spousal support, and alimony in your state, and question everything your lawyer tells you. Lawyers are in business to make money. Also, ask friends for their input and experience in getting a divorce. Friends can also recommend a great divorce lawyer.

Remember that the bisexual partner who does not come out of the closet will be a persuasive blamer and will do anything to protect himself. His goal is to humiliate you publicly and use anything he can against you.

Mary's partner, the blamer, would have used anything against her. He publicly humiliated her and spread rumors about her. Jake resorted to all kinds of misdeeds and outrageous behavior to save the face that wears a mask. He is a bisexual, narcissistic sex addict and unable truly to exhibit care and compassion for another.

NOTES

12
LESSONS LEARNED

The lessons Mary learned were monumental, as was the education she received about a bisexual partner who does not come out of the closet, gaslighting and narcissism. She was fortunate to have a psychiatrist and a therapist to help her through the uncover, discovery and recovery process. Mary learned many lessons along the way:

- Jake used and abused her behind closed doors and that he covered up this behavior with his personality traits.
- The divorce process in this type of situation is dramatic and traumatic.
- She learned how the grieving process works.
- She learned to honor her gut feelings (intuition) and her head. The heart is emotional, so women need to be tough.

- Many women in the same situation try to handle the trauma on their own; some end up hanging on to the past.
- She learned to move toward the future with new activities and interests.
- Her life would forever change.
- Forgiveness and acceptance are a process that requires patience and perseverance.
- The narcissistic personality plays a significant role in the life of a bisexual partner who does not come out of the closet.
- Although Jake was in the closet, she, too, had been in the closet, hiding from this nightmare in denial.
- She learned to seek help from professionals.
- Many people you love abandon you in your time of need. They just do not understand or want to

believe such an atrocity has taken place.

- It is important to believe people when they come forward about a significant other's sexuality.

- She could use the Internet to gather information about bisexuality.

- She had to replace low self-esteem with high self-esteem so as not to attract another bisexual. For Mary, this is a work in progress.

- She learned to love herself; she no longer needs validation by a man.

- Mary learned to make new friends who believe in her and her story.

- She learned to live alone and not be lonely.

- She learned to meditate and trust that the universe would take her where she needed to go.

- She learned to use the library as a resource.
- She learned to share her story and learn from others about bisexual partners.
- A bisexual may never come out of the closet, but she can.
- In time, the rapist of her heart would stop intimidating her.
- Love can dominate over fear, and she did not have to be afraid.
- She did not need to blame herself for Jake being bisexual. Mary thought she was at fault; she thought she turned him into a bisexual.
- When belittled, acknowledge the sick feeling in your stomach. Your self-esteem is being eroded. Violence is occurring.
- When you suspect something is wrong, it is not your imagination.
- She is a survivor.

- She learned about sex addiction and post-traumatic stress disorder.
- She learned about the cycle of violence and bisexual characteristics.
- She is not alone.
- The number of gay, lesbian, bisexual, and transgender adults is estimated to be one in ten.
- Mary became aware of the clues that were so vivid.
- Although Jake was a sex addict, she was a love addict bound to him in betrayal.

Jake had shattered Mary's heart. Jake convinced her friends and her children that she fabricated the story of being married to a bisexual. Mary remains in recovery. Mary's perseverance to learn and grow to move forward is beautiful. She has moved from discovery to recovery. Now she is working on thriving.

NOTES

CLOSURE

Life takes some crazy directions sometimes,
Causing changes, we cannot hope to
anticipate.

Even though we try to cope,
Some things are beyond our control.
We can only accept them and move forward
As best, we can.

WEBSITES

http://www.ismyhusbandbisexual.com

www.spectorsoft.com/
You can order spyware for the computer your husband uses to detect e-mail, websites, chat rooms, and instant messages.

http://signsofabisexualhusband.com

http://en.wikipedia.org/wiki/Bisexuality

http://iub.edu/~kinsey/research/ak-hhscale.html

http://sexaddictionhelp.com

http://BonnieKayeBooks.com

http://en.wikipedia.org/wiki/K%C3%BCbler-Ross_model

http://www.gayhusbands.com

http://en.wikipedia.org/wiki/Psychological_ab
use

http://domestic-violence.laws.com/domestic-
abuse

http://gaylife.about.com/

http://gaylife.about.com/od/comingout/a/popu
lation.htm

http://webmd.com/anxiety-panic/guide/post-
traumatic-stress-disorder

http://www.ncbi.nih.gov/pubmedhealth/PMH
0001923/

http://en.wikipedia.org/wiki/Gaslighting

http://voices.yahoo.com/crazy-making-form-
emotional-psychological-abuse-7078566.html

http://omgrey.wordpress.com/2011/05/18/brea
king-the-betrayal-bond/

http://www.sexhelp.com/am-i-a-sex-addict

http://marriage.about.com/od/communication
keys/g/stonewalling.htm

BIBLIOGRAPHY

American Psychiatric Association (APA). Diagnostic and Statistical Manual of Mental Disorders: DSM IV, 4th ed. Washington, DC: American Psychiatric Publishing, 2000.

Bloomfield, Harold, Melba Colgrove, and Peter McWilliams. How to Survive the Loss of a Love. Allen Park, MI: Prelude Press/Mary Books, 1992.

Carnes, Patrick. Don't Call It Love: Recovery from Sexual Addiction. New York: Bantam Books, 1991.

Carnes, Patrick. Out of the Shadows: Understanding Sexual Addiction. Center City, MN: Hazelden, 2001.

Carnes, Patrick. The Betrayal Bond. Health Communications, 2010.

Cram, Heather. You're What?! Minneapolis, MN: Bascom Hill, 2008.

Dutton, D. G. The Abusive Personality: Violence and Control in Intimate Relationships, 2nd ed. New York: Guilford Press, 2007.

Eddy, William, and Randi Kreger. Splitting: Protecting Yourself While Divorcing Someone with Borderline or Narcissistic Personality Disorder. Oakland, CA: New Harbinger, 2011.

Elliott, Susan. Getting Past Your Breakup: How to Turn a Devastating Loss into the Best Thing That Ever Happened to You. Cambridge, MA: Da Capo Press, 2009.

Goulston, Mark. Post-Traumatic Stress Disorder for Dummies. Wiley Publishing, 2007.

Grever, Carol. My Husband is Gay. Berkeley, CA: Crossing Press, 2001.

Hill, Ivan. The Bisexual Spouse. New York: Harper and Row, 1987.

Kaye, Bonnie. The Gay Husband Checklist. British Columbia: CCB Publishing, 2008.

Kaye, Bonnie, and Doug Dittmer. Over the Cliff. British Columbia: CCB Publishing, 2011.

King, J. L. On the Down Low. New York: Harlem Moon, 2005.

Mellody, Pia. Facing Love Addiction. New York: HarperCollins Publishers, 1992.

Schaef, Anne Wilson. Escape From Intimacy. New York: Harper Collins Publishers, 1989.

Schaeffer, Brenda. Is it Love or is it Addiction? Center City, MN: Hazelden, 1997.

Schiraldi, Glenn. The Post-Traumatic Stress Disorder Sourcebook: A Guide to Healing. New York: McGraw-Hill, 2009.

Schore, A. N. Affect Regulation and the Repair of the Self. New York: W. W. Norton and Company, 2003.

Williams, Mary Beth, and Soili Poijula. The PTSD Workbook: Simple, Effective Techniques for Overcoming Traumatic Stress Symptoms. Oakland, CA: New Harbinger Publications, 2013.